**Profitable Applications
of the Break-Even System**

Profitable Applications
of the Break-Even System

Carl L. Moore

Prentice-Hall, Inc.
Englewood Cliffs, N. J.

PRENTICE-HALL INTERNATIONAL, INC., *London*
PRENTICE-HALL OF AUSTRALIA, PTY. LTD., *Sydney*
PRENTICE-HALL OF CANADA, LTD., *Toronto*
PRENTICE-HALL OF INDIA PRIVATE LTD., *New Delhi*
PRENTICE-HALL OF JAPAN, INC., *Tokyo*

©1971 BY

PRENTICE-HALL, INC.
ENGLEWOOD CLIFFS, N.J.

LIBRARY OF CONGRESS
CATALOG CARD NUMBER: 75-141497

Second Printing.....June, 1972

PRINTED IN THE UNITED STATES OF AMERICA
ISBN–O-13-726646-4
B&P

DEDICATION

To my wife Ruth

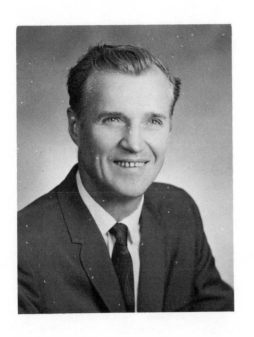

About the Author

Carl L. Moore is Professor of Accounting at Lehigh University. He is an author with Robert K. Jaedicke of Stanford University of two editions of *Managerial Accounting* published by South-Western Publishing Company. He has also written articles for technical journals and a case that has been published in two different management textbooks.

The author has had over twenty years of experience in education, industrial accounting, and public accounting. In addition, he has been an adviser and consultant for various companies and organizations.

Professor Moore received an A.B. Degree in Economics from Bucknell University and an M.A. Degree in Accounting from the University of Pittsburgh. He is also a Certified Public Accountant in Pennsylvania.

Carl Moore is a member of the Pennsylvania Institute of Certified Public Accountants, the National Association of Accountants, the American Accounting Association, Phi Beta Kappa, Beta Gamma Sigma, Beta Alpha Psi, and Alpha Kappa Psi.

He is listed in *Contemporary Authors* and in *Who's Who in the East.*

How This Book Can Help You

This book shows how the relatively simple concept of a break-even point can be enlarged and put to use in the control of costs, in the selection of the best economic alternative, and in making decisions and plans in virtually every vital area of business endeavor. Essentially the break-even point is a point of balance—a balance between the advantages and disadvantages of any course of action. The balancing point is a guide that can be applied in obtaining a better control over operations and in improving the planning and decision-making process. Several applications are discussed and illustrated to stimulate your thinking and to give ideas that can be applied in your own business situation.

The action techniques—clearly explained and illustrated—apply not only to the conventional business enterprise but also to the non-profit organization. Accountants, financial control officers, and cost analysts can make better decisions by putting into effect the break-even strategies in this book. Business executives at all levels and in all functional areas, extending from the president to the various departmental supervisors, can benefit from this general approach and the derived practical applications.

The material is presented concisely in a logical sequence. All technical terms are defined briefly and clearly so that the book can be read with relative ease even though you may have had little or no formal training in accounting.

HOW THE BOOK IS ORGANIZED

There are 14 chapters. The first chapter explains the *one* basic principle that supports the break-even concept, and the next chapter shows you how profit plans can be presented in the form of helpful visual aids that will call attention to the essential features. In Chapter 3 the problem of segregating costs according to how they vary with changes in the volume of activity is discussed and explained carefully with accompanying illustrations. This important analytical process is presented early in the book because it is essential not only in conventional break-even analysis but also in budgeting, in planning operations, and in controlling costs.

In subsequent chapters the break-even principle is expanded to show you how it applies to many vital areas of business administration. For example, the fourth chapter shows how profits can be reported to emphasize the relationship between sales volume and profits. This method of reporting profits is compared with the conventional method, and the benefits to be derived from each method are set forth clearly.

The next three chapters deal with cost control. The first of these three chapters shows how costs can be controlled in general, and the next two chapters give specific steps for handling materials costs and the costs of selling and distribution so that costs can be held to a minimum with no sacrifice of essential services to customers. Vital business decision areas are discussed in the next six chapters, with a chapter each on the combination of profitable product lines, pricing differentials, the extent of the business operation, the current resources required to support the level of business activity, the selection of the best capital investment alternative, and the financing decision. Finally, a chapter is given to show how the techniques of break-even analysis can be applied specifically to help solve the business problems faced by the manager of a non-profit organization.

Technical terms are carefully defined in each chapter, and theory is discussed only to the extent necessary for an understanding of the applications. Illustrations and examples are given throughout the book not only to make it easier for you to grasp the essential points but also to show you how you can put these principles to work in your own particular areas of interest.

For example, Chapter 8 is entitled "Selecting the Most Lucrative Product Lines," and early in the chapter the general problem area is discussed briefly. Terms that may be unfamiliar to the reader are also carefully defined. Then an example is given to show how this type of decisional analysis is essentially an extended version of basic break-even analysis. Points that require special attention are identified, and illustrations are given to show how information can be organized and used in making a decision.

Again, in Chapter 12, "Selecting the Best Capital Investment Alternative," the capital investment itself is defined, and the type of decision facing the company is set forth clearly. Factors to be used in the analysis are defined with interrelationships fully explained. The essential data required for the analysis are identified, and suggestions are given for the collection of these data. A straightforward method that can be used for various investment situations is explained briefly with accompanying illustrations. As an aid in interpreting the results, it is suggested that a visual form of presentation may be helpful; and directions are given for the preparation of this visual aid.

HOW TO BENEFIT FROM THIS BOOK

It is suggested that the book should first be read in its entirety to get a feeling for the underlying theme that runs throughout the text. After your thoughts have been focused on this basic principle of break-even analysis, consider the problems that are of primary concern to you and then consider ways in which you can adapt this principle to meet your own particular needs.

Refer back to those chapters that deal more specifically with your areas of interest. Reread these chapters and sort out the material that has a more direct bearing on your problem. Then examine your present method of operation critically, deciding what steps you may want to take to refine your techniques—steps that may simplify your work and improve results.

Suppose, for example, that you are particularly interested in the control of departmental manufacturing costs. If costs deviate from the expected pattern, you may want to find out why so that you can take steps to correct an unfavorable condition. Yet, you recognize the fact that an investigation will be time consuming and will also add to costs. How can you decide when to investigate a cost variance and when to ignore it? A certain amount of variation can be expected in the normal course of operations. On the other hand, the variation may result from some abnormality that should be corrected before cost variations have time to accumulate. This important problem is given full attention in Chapter 5, "Improving Profits By Better Cost Control."

Or you may be interested in the improvement of profits through an extension of your present operation. As a manufacturer, you may be considering the production of components used in one of your product lines, or you may want to extend the manufacturing operation by producing an improved version of a present product line. What are some of the factors that bear on this decision? How can these factors be brought together to help you make the right decision? This type of problem is examined closely in Chapter 10, "Deciding Whether to Extend or Contract Operations."

There will be situations where you will feel that you are completely blocked by factors that seemingly cannot be expressed in dollars. How can a value be placed on a factor that appears to defy every attempt to measure it in dollars? Human values, for example, are difficult to measure in terms of money. Yet it is possible to get indirectly an approximate answer that will balance human needs against available resources. This type of problem is brought up in various chapters and is given more specific attention in Chapter 14, "Break-Even Applications in the Non-Profit Organization."

Carl L. Moore

ACKNOWLEDGMENTS

The author expresses gratitude to Professors James B. Hobbs, Jon T. Innes, Eli Schwartz, Wendell P. Trumbull, and Andrew R. Weintraub of the College of Business and Economics of Lehigh University for helpful suggestions and to Nan C. Fahy for typing the manuscript. Special recognition is given to Lao Russell and the late Walter Russell of the University of Science and Philosophy for general guidance that led to the publication of this book.

TABLE OF CONTENTS

1

A Quick Look
at the Break-Even Concept

The principle of balance is evident in nature and also in the successful operation of business. In fact, an important financial statement that depicts the financial position of a business is designated as the balance sheet. The accounting process itself is a balanced operation whereby each transaction is recorded by a self-checking system with one part of a transaction being balanced by the other part of it. Double-entry accounting provides a control over mechanical accuracy through the balancing principle and is a logical system for organizing and processing financial data.

The concept of balance in business is not a peculiarity of the accounting function but is pertinent to all areas of business endeavor. Balance in itself is not an objective, of course, but it is a means by which objectives can be attained.

ORGANIZATIONAL OBJECTIVES

Business organizations and other organizations establish central objectives, and efforts are directed toward the fulfillment of these objectives. Examples of these primary or central objectives are given below.

(1) A business enterprise seeks profits that will provide a socially acceptable rate of return on investment.

(2) A government attempts to provide services to the citizens at an acceptable cost.

(3) A non-profit organization works toward the satisfaction of a general or specific need in our society.

The economic considerations are of secondary importance to the non-profit entity; this may be true in certain circumstances for both the business type of entity and the non-profit entity. In any case, the economic factors cannot be entirely ignored as long as resources are scarce in relation to human desires and needs.

19

THE BREAK-EVEN POINT

A business enterprise expects profits, profits that are satisfactory to all concerned. In the preliminary stages of profit planning, a businessman estimates the amount of revenue that must be realized to cover all expenses. When revenue is equal to expenses, there is neither profit nor loss. The point of balance where there is neither profit nor loss is called the *break-even point*.

The break-even point is obviously not a desired point of balance. Instead, it is a reference point that can be used in further planning. The break-even point is illustrated in Figure 1-1 as a point of balance by a simple set of scales.

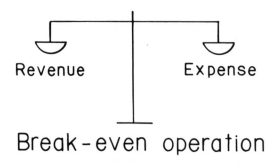

Figure 1-1

Business, however, does not merely seek a balance between revenue and expense. The objective is to earn profits. Seemingly, the addition of profits will destroy the balance. There are those who believe that profits are a surplus, an unnecessary excess. This theory overlooks the fact that all factors engaged in the production and distribution of goods and services must receive a fair return if there is to be a *stabilized balance,* a balance of true equilibrium. A society must provide for profit whether the term "profit" is used or not. Without a fair distribution to all factors, a society will destroy itself through a lack of balance.

The illustration of the scales is presented in Figure 1-2 with socially desirable profits included to bring the scales into a stabilized state of balance.

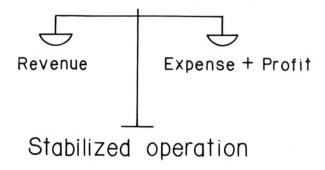

Figure 1-2

THE FUNDAMENTAL BREAK-EVEN EQUATION

At this time, attention will be directed to the first step; that is, solving for the break-even point of zero profitability. The revenue that is required to break even, or, stated in another way, the number of units that must be sold to produce that revenue, can be computed from a simple equation.

$$\text{Revenue} = \text{Expense}$$
or
$$\text{Revenue} - \text{Expense} = 0.$$

EXPENSES CLASSIFIED BY BEHAVIOR PATTERNS

Before the break-even point can be determined, all expenses must be classified according to their behavior with respect to changes in the volume of sales or with respect to changes in the level of operating activity. The expenses must be classified either as variable expenses or as fixed expenses. This distinction is very important in arriving at a valid solution. *Variable expenses* are those expenses that increase or decrease proportionately with changes in volume of sales or changes in level of activity. The cost of merchandise sold is an example of a variable cost. A merchant can buy the product he sells at a cost of $2 a unit. If he sells one unit of this product, his cost of goods sold is $2. If he sells two units, the cost of goods sold is $4; and if he sells three units, it is $6, etc. For each additional unit sold, there is an additional cost of goods sold of $2. A *fixed expense,* on the other hand, is an expense that does not change as a result of changes in the volume of sales or in the level of operating activity. The merchant may have property taxes of $500 a year. Property taxes will not be affected by sales volume or level of business activity. They will be $500 whether the merchant sells one unit or a thousand units of product during the year.

Many expenses will not fit the rigid definition given for variable expenses. They will vary with changes in sales volume or level of activity, but they will not vary proportionately. Maintenance of equipment, for example, may increase as the equipment is used more intensively to produce more sales. It is unlikely, however, that the expense will increase in *proportion* to the increase in sales. Maintenance expense may be $3,000 a year regardless of the level of activity and may increase at the rate of $3 a unit for the first 100 units sold, increase to $4 a unit for the next 100 units sold, and increase to $5 a unit for an additional 100 units sold. Expenses that have both variable and fixed characteristics are called *semivariable expenses.*

The semivariable expenses must be analyzed carefully and segregated into variable and fixed portions before they can be used in break-even analysis. The methods used to segregate these costs will be discussed in Chapter 3. At this stage of development, it is assumed that all expenses have been properly classified as being either variable or fixed expenses.

AN EXPANDED BREAK-EVEN EQUATION

The break-even equation may be stated as shown below.

$$\text{Revenue} = \text{Variable expenses} + \text{Fixed expenses}$$
or
$$\text{Revenue} - \text{Variable expenses} = \text{Fixed expenses.}$$

The revenue as reduced by the variable expenses is designated as the *contribution margin*. Contribution margin has sometimes been defined as the profit contribution of a particular segment of the business to the total business operation. This profit contribution is equal to the revenue reduced by the sum of the variable expenses and the fixed expenses incremental to the business segment in question. In this book, however, contribution margin is defined as the excess of revenue over the variable expenses only.

The contribution margin concept is illustrated below. Assume that sales revenue amounts to $250,000 for the year and that the variable expenses to produce and sell the product amount to $150,000. The contribution margin, that is, the excess of revenue over variable expenses, is $100,000.

Revenue	$250,000
Variable expenses	150,000
Contribution margin	$100,000

The contribution margin as the excess of revenue over variable expenses is the amount available for the recovery of the fixed expenses and for the realization of profits.

In the equation given below, *Contribution margin* is substituted for the expression *Revenue - Variable expenses.*

Contribution margin = Fixed expenses.

If the total contribution margin is equal to the fixed expenses, the business entity breaks even. It is possible to solve for the number of units that must be sold in order to break even if the fixed expenses are given and if the contribution margin per unit of product can be computed.

Assume, for example, that fixed expenses for the year are estimated at $60,000. Each unit of product sells for $25, and the variable expenses are equal to $15 per unit of product.

Unit revenue	$25
Unit variable expenses	15
Unit contribution margin	$10

The break-even equation appears below.

Contribution margin (total)

Number of units sold X Unit contribution margin = Fixed expenses.

Solve for the number of units that must be sold in order to break even.

$$\text{Number of units sold} = \frac{\text{Fixed expenses}}{\text{Unit contribution margin}} .$$

$$\text{Number of units sold} = \frac{\$60,000}{\$10} .$$

Number of units sold = 6,000 .

In order to break even, 6,000 units of product must be sold. Expressed in terms of sales revenue, the revenue at break-even point must be $150,000 ($25 unit selling price X 6,000 units).

Sales revenue can also be computed directly by expressing the contribution margin as a percentage of sales revenue.

	Dollars	Percentages
Unit revenue	$25	100%
Unit variable expenses	15	60
Unit contribution margin	$10	40%

The break-even equation is slightly revised as follows:

Sales revenue x Contribution margin percentage = Fixed expenses.

$$\text{Sales revenue} = \frac{\text{Fixed expenses}}{\text{Contribution margin percentage}}$$

$$\text{Sales revenue} = \frac{\$60,000}{.4}$$

$$\text{Sales revenue} = \$150,000 \ .$$

The break-even solution can be proved quite easily as shown below.

Sales revenue	$150,000
Variable expenses, 60% of sales revenue	90,000
Contribution margin	$60,000
Fixed expenses	60,000
Break-even point (no profit or loss)	-0-

PROFITS AND BREAK-EVEN ANALYSIS

As stated earlier, the break-even point is merely a reference point for planning operations. A more stable balance is achieved when a desired profit has been realized. The desired profit is handled in the equation as if it were an additional fixed expense.

Number of units sold x Unit contribution margin = Fixed expenses + Desired profit.

Using the data from the previous example, assume that the desired profit is to be $90,000.

$$\text{Number of units sold} = \frac{\text{Fixed expenses} + \text{Desired profit}}{\text{Unit contribution margin}}$$

$$\text{Number of units sold} = \frac{\$60,000 + \$90,000}{\$10}$$

$$\text{Number of units sold} = \frac{\$150,000}{\$10}$$

$$\text{Number of units sold} = 15,000.$$

The sales revenue is $375,000 ($25 unit selling price. X 15,000 units). A proof of the solution is given below.

Sales revenue	$375,000
Variable expenses, 60% of sales revenue	225,000
Contribution margin	$150,000
Fixed expenses	60,000
Net income	$ 90,000

DESIRED PROFITS AND INCOME TAXES

In the example given, no provision was made for income taxes. The net income of $90,000 is the net income *before* income taxes. The net income remaining for the business, that is, the final net income, will be less than $90,000 by the amount of the income taxes.

Assume that the net income is expected to be $90,000 *after* income taxes. The break-even equation will have to be revised to allow for the effect of the income tax. If the income tax rate is 40 percent, the business entity must earn enough profit before tax to cover the 40 percent tax and have a balance remaining that is equal to $90,000. If 40 percent of the profit before taxes must be applied to income taxes, then 60 percent of this profit is left for the business. The desired profit after income taxes is equal to 60 percent of the profit before income taxes. The profit before income taxes is computed as follows:

$$\text{Profit before income taxes} = \frac{\$90,000 \text{ profit after income taxes}}{60\% \text{ portion remaining for the business.}}$$

$$\text{Profit before income taxes} = \$150,000.$$

This computation can be made quite easily within the framework of the break-even equation. The profit before income taxes is equal to the profit after income taxes divided by the complement of the income tax rate. The complement of the income tax rate is the percentage of profit before taxes that is retained by the business.

$$100\% \text{ profit before taxes} - 40\% \text{ tax rate} = 60\% \text{ profit after taxes.}$$

The break-even equation as revised is given below.

$$\text{Number of units sold} = \frac{\text{Fixed expenses} + \dfrac{\text{Desired profit after income taxes}}{\text{Complement of the income tax rate}}}{\text{Unit contribution margin}}$$

$$\text{Number of units sold} = \frac{\$60,000 + \dfrac{\$90,000}{.6}}{\$10}$$

$$\text{Number of units sold} = 21,000 \ .$$

A proof of the solution follows:

Sales revenue (21,000 units X $25 unit selling price)	$525,000
Variable expenses (60% of sales revenue)	315,000
Contribution margin	$210,000
Fixed expenses	60,000
Net income before income taxes	$150,000
Income taxes—40% of $150,000	60,000
Net income after income taxes	$ 90,000

TWO OR MORE PRODUCT LINES

If only one line of product is produced and sold, it will be possible to compute the number of units that must be sold in order to break even or to realize a given amount of profit after income taxes. However, when more than one line of product is handled, the combined product sales expressed in physical units may have no significance. With a combination of products, break-even sales may be expressed in dollars of revenue based on the assumption that the various product lines will be sold in a given proportion.

Assume that a company sells three product lines. Based on past experience and estimates for the next year, it is anticipated that 60 percent of the total sales revenue will be provided by Product A with the remaining 40 percent furnished equally by Products B and C.

The variable expenses expressed as a percentage of sales revenue for each product line are set forth below.

Product lines	Variable expenses, percentage of revenue
A	75
B	25
C	50

If the product lines are sold in the expected proportions, the percentage of total variable expenses to total sales revenue can be computed as follows:

Product lines	Percentages of total revenue		Variable expenses, percentage of revenue		Variable expenses, weighted percentage of revenue
A	.6	X	.75	=	.45
B	.2	X	.25	=	.05
C	.2	X	.50	=	.10
				Total	.60

On a combined basis with product lines sold in a fixed proportion, the variable expenses in total should be equal to 60 percent of sales revenue. The contribution margin in total should then be equal to 40 percent of sales revenue. With fixed expenses of $120,000 for the year, the company should be able to break even with a total sales revenue of $300,000.

$$\text{Sales revenue at break-even point} = \frac{\text{Fixed expenses}}{\text{Weighted contribution margin percentage}}$$

$$\text{Sales revenue at break-even point} = \frac{\$120,000}{.4}$$

$$\text{Sales revenue at break-even point} = \$300,000$$

Combined sales revenue	$300,000
Variable expenses (60% of revenue)	180,000
Contribution margin (weighted average)	$120,000
Fixed expenses	120,000
Break-even point (no profit or loss)	-0-

The sales revenue from each line of product at the break-even point can be derived from the total revenue.

Product lines	Percentage of revenue, each line		Total revenue		Revenue, each line
A	60%	X	$300,000	=	$180,000
B	20	X	300,000	=	60,000
C	20	X	300,000	=	60,000
	100%				$300,000

The number of units of each line that must be sold can be calculated easily by dividing the revenue from each line by its unit selling price. For example, Product A sells at a price of $12 each pound, Product B sells at a price of $20 per unit, and Product C sells at a price of $5 per foot. The number of units to be sold is computed below.

Product lines	Revenue	Unit selling prices	Number of units
A	$180,000	$12 @ lb.	15,000 lbs.
B	60,000	20 @ unit	3,000 units
C	60,000	5 @ foot	12,000 ft.
	$300,000		

SUMMARY

The concept of a balancing point is frequently employed in business operations. At the initial stages of profit planning, for example, management will determine the amount of revenue that must be realized if all expenses are to be recovered. The point where there is neither profit nor loss is called the break-even point, and this point can be determined by the use of a simple equation. A more meaningful balance, a balance of stability, is attained when a business not only breaks even but realized a desired profit on operations. The number of units of product that must be sold or the revenue required to earn a desired profit can also be determined by using an expanded form of the break-even equation.

2

Visual Aids
in Profit Planning

Visual representations in the form of graphs and charts are often used to show what profits will be under given conditions and to call attention to the influence of changes in the sales volume, prices, costs, and the composition of sales. These visual aids are built upon the fundamental principle of the break-even equation. The break-even equation in itself is useful in a limited way, but it cannot convey ideas as quickly as graphs or charts. Furthermore, any particular equation is based upon a given set of values for the factors and cannot show the complete picture of profits for various levels of activity. A graph or a chart shows at a glance what may be expected over the entire range of operating activity.

THE BREAK-EVEN CHART

A break-even chart is often used to show how revenues and expenses change with changes in sales volume and to indicate the profits or losses that may be expected for various levels of sales. Sales expressed in units of product are shown on the horizontal scale of a two-dimensional graph with dollars given on the vertical scale. Both revenues and expenses are plotted for the various numbers of units sold. The revenue points are connected by a line, and a similar line is drawn to connect the expenses. The company breaks even at the point where the two lines intersect. The lines themselves show how both revenues and expenses increase with increases in sales volume. A profit or loss is measured as the distance between the lines at any given volume of sales.

The break-even chart is illustrated in Figure 2-1 by assuming that one line of product is sold for $6 a unit with variable expenses of $3 a unit and total fixed expenses for the year of $60,000. Sales volume ranging from 10,000 to 50,000 units is given in 10,000-unit intervals.

Break-Even Chart

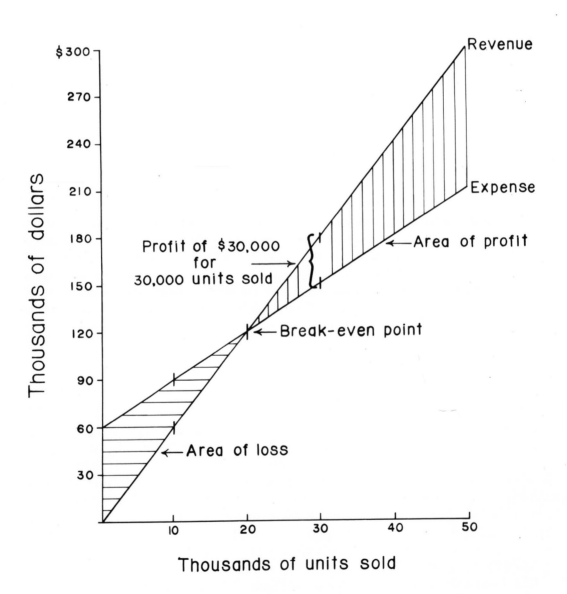

Figure 2-1

The revenues and expenses have been plotted from the computations given below.

Thousands of units sold	10	20	30
Revenue ($6 per unit)	$ 60,000	$120,000	$180,000
Expenses:			
Variable ($3 per unit)	$ 30,000	$ 60,000	$ 90,000
Fixed	60,000	60,000	60,000
Total expenses	$ 90,000	$120,000	$150,000
Net profit (loss)	($ 30,000)	-0-	$ 30,000

Thousands of units sold	40	50
Revenue ($6 per unit)	$240,000	$300,000
Expenses:		
Variable ($3 per unit)	$120,000	$150,000
Fixed	60,000	60,000
Total expenses	$180,000	$210,000
Net profit (loss)	$ 60,000	$ 90,000

When 20,000 units are sold, the company breaks even as indicated by the intersection of the revenue and expense lines. A profit of $30,000 is earned when 30,000 units are sold. This is measured on the chart as the difference between the revenue of $180,000 and the expense of $150,000 at the 30,000-unit level.

EXPENSE DETAIL ON THE BREAK-EVEN CHART

A break-even chart may also be drawn to show the expenses broken down as to behavior and function. This type of presentation measures the amount of a particular expense classification at any sales level and shows how the expense is affected by changes in sales volume. Using data from the last illustration, assume that the variable expense of $3 per unit consists of $2 for the cost of the product and $1 for selling expenses. The fixed expenses of $60,000 consist of $40,000 for the selling function and $20,000 for the administrative function.

The break-even chart with expense detail is illustrated for the reader in Figure 2-2. The chart shows that the variable expenses begin at zero and increase as volume of sales increases. The fixed expenses, on the other hand, are the same whether any units are sold or not. If desired, of course, the expenses could be detailed even further.

Break-Even Chart

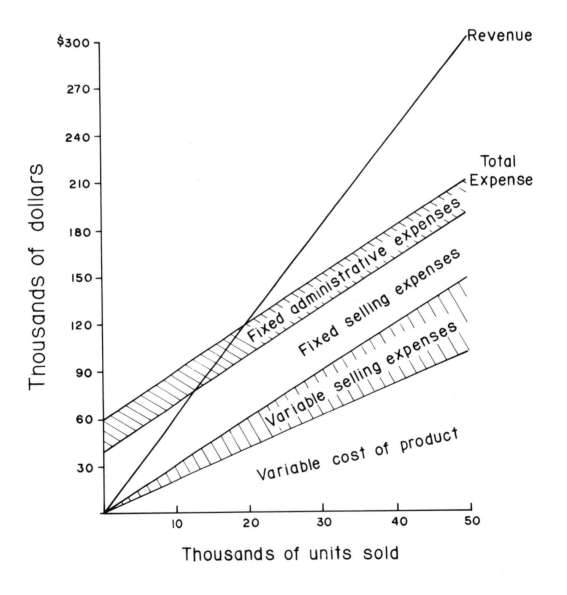

Figure 2-2

VARIATIONS IN PRICE AND EXPENSE

In the illustration it has been assumed that all units can be sold at a given price of $6 per unit and that the variable expense will always increase by $3 per unit. This may or may not be true in practice. Prices and expenses may increase but not at a constant rate.

The economist uses the term *marginal revenue,* and defines it as the additional revenue realized from the sale of one more unit of product. As more units are offered for sale on the market, the price may have to be reduced if all of the units are to be sold. If the price is reduced to sell greater volume, the marginal revenue (the amount of revenue added by the sale of an additional unit– will decrease as more units are sold. Total revenue will increase but at a decreasing rate. For example, it may be possible to sell one unit of product for $100. In order to sell the second unit, it may be necessary to reduce the price to $80. A third unit can be sold for $60, and a fourth unit can be sold for $40.

The economist uses the term *marginal cost,* and defines it as the additional cost to produce and sell one more unit of product. As more units are produced and sold, the cost to produce and sell each additional unit will decrease as economies are derived from a larger scale operation. Fixed expenses, for example, will be spread over a larger number of units, thus reducing the cost per unit. Eventually, however, the cost to produce and sell an additional unit will increase when production and sales exceed an economic level of operation for the existing facilities. Assume that it cost $50 to produce and sell the one unit in the example given above. The marginal cost of the second unit is $40 (the additional cost of this unit), and the marginal cost of the third unit is $30. The fourth unit, however, adds $40 to cost. Apparently, the business has gone beyond its most economic level of operation.

	Per unit		Total		
Number of units sold	Marginal revenue	Marginal cost	Revenue	Cost	Profit (or loss)
1	$100	$50	$100	$50	$50
2	80	40	180	90	90
3	60	30	240	120	120
4	40	40	280	160	120

The business should continue to produce and sell units up to a point where the marginal revenue is equal to the marginal cost. Additional profits can be earned up to this point. In the example, marginal revenue and marginal cost are equal when four units are sold. Obviously, it will not pay to continue operations when the price at which an article can be sold is equal to the cost of making and selling it.

If the revenues and expenses do not vary at a constant rate over the range of operations, the revenue and expense lines on a break-even chart will not be straight lines. On the break-even chart in Figure 2-3, revenue increases at a decreasing rate as shown by the curve, and the expense curve sweeps upward at an increasing rate.

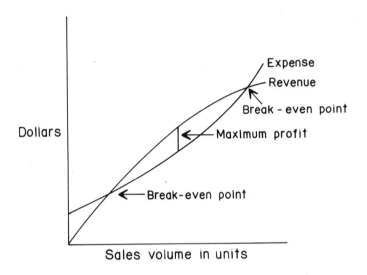

Figure 2-3

There are two break-even points in the example given. The business can maximize profits by operating beyond the first break-even point where the spread between the revenue and expense lines is greatest.

Ordinarily, in preparing a break-even chart, an accountant assumes that operations are conducted within a range where all production can be sold at a given price with total expenses increasing at a constant rate. If this is true, revenue and expense lines will be straight lines. On the other hand, if the selling price must be reduced to sell additional volume or if expenses increase at an increasing rate, the lines on the break-even chart will have to be drawn accordingly.

THE PROFIT-VOLUME GRAPH

The profit-volume graph, or P/V graph as it is sometimes called, is another form of graphic presentation that may be used instead of or in conjunction with the break-even chart. The profit-volume graph is neither superior nor inferior to the break-even chart. The selection of a method of presentation depends upon the type of information desired and individual preference. The profit-volume graph may be preferred in many cases because of its relative simplicity. Less lines are plotted, thus making it easier to read the basic information directly from the graph.

Sales volume is depicted along the horizontal axis of the P/V graph; and the vertical axis is divided into two parts by a horizontal line that serves as a break-even line, a line of zero profitability. Above this line dollars of profit are measured on the vertical scale, and below it dollars of loss are measured. Profits and losses are plotted on the graph at various sales volumes and are connected by a line designated as the profit line.

A P/V graph (Figure 2-4) is given for a line of product selling for $30 a unit with a variable unit cost of $20 and total fixed expenses for the year of $300,000. Sales volume is given in 10,000-unit intervals ranging from 10,000 units to 80,000 units.

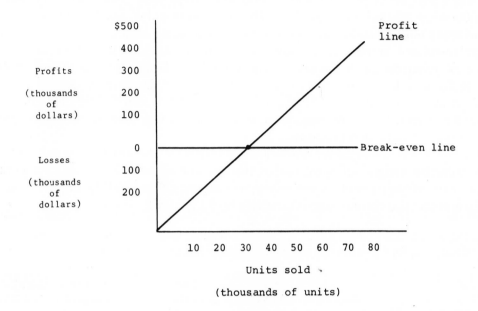

Figure 2-4

Profits and losses can be read directly from the P/V graph and are not measured as the distance between the revenue and expense lines as was the case with the break-even chart. For example, there is a loss of $100,000 if only 20,000 units are sold. This can be read directly from the vertical scale. The business breaks even when 30,000 units are sold. A profit of $300,000 is earned when 60,000 units are sold.

AN INCREASE OR DECREASE IN UNIT VARIABLE COST

The slope of the profit line changes with changes in the unit variable cost. If the unit variable cost increases, the contribution margin is reduced and, of course, the profit from the sale of a given number of units is lower. Conversely, with a decrease in unit variable cost, there is an increase in the contribution margin with higher profits for a given volume of sales.

Using the data from the previous example, assume that the selling price per unit remains at $30 and that the variable unit cost increases from $20 to $25. The fixed expenses for the year remain at $300,000. For each unit sold, the contribution margin has been reduced from $10 a unit to $5 a unit. The contribution margin is only half of what it was before. Therefore, twice as many units will have to be sold to earn the same profits as before.

The original profit picture can be compared with the revised profit picture on the same P/V graph shown in Figure 2-5.

Note that both lines begin at an origin of $300,000, the amount of the fixed expenses. If no units are sold, the loss is equal to the fixed expenses of $300,000. With an increase in unit variable cost, the revised profit line rises at a slower rate. Originally, there was a loss of $100,000 when 20,000 units were sold. Now there is a loss of $100,000 when 40,000 units are sold. The break-even point was 30,000 units. Now twice as many units (60,000) must be sold in order to break even.

A profit-volume graph clearly shows what can be expected if unit variable costs increase. A relatively small increase in the variable cost per unit can reduce profits substantially in a large-scale operation. For example, an increase in variable cost of only a penny a unit can reduce total profits by $50,000 a year if 5,000,000 units are produced and sold. It is quite easy, then, to understand why management places great emphasis on cost reduction programs.

If the contribution margin per unit is already relatively low, any further reduction in the contribution margin will yield profits that are considerably lower on a percentage basis. In each of the examples given below, it is assumed that 100,000 units of product are sold and that the variable cost is increased by $1 per unit.

1. The original contribution margin percentage is reduced from 50 percent to 49 percent.
   Result: The total contribution margin in dollars is reduced by 2 percent.

	Selling price	Unit variable cost	Unit contribution margin	Contribution margin percentage
Original basis	$100	$50	$50	50%
Increased variable cost	100	51	49	49

	Total contribution margin	Pct. reduction in contribution margin
Original basis	$5,000,000	—
Increased variable cost	$4,900,000	2%

2. The original contribution margin percentage is reduced from 20 percent to 10 percent.
   Result: The total contribution margin in dollars is reduced by 50 percent.

	Selling price	Unit variable cost	Unit contribution margin	Contribution margin percentage
Original basis	$10	$8	$2	20%
Increased variable cost	10	9	1	10

P/V Graph

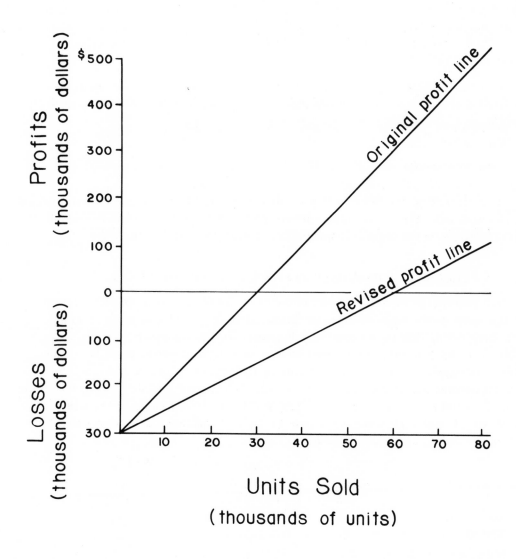

Figure 2-5

	Total contribution margin	Pct. reduction in contribution margin
Original basis	$200,000	——
Increased variable cost	100,000	50%

PRICE CHANGES

The slope of the profit line also changes as a result of changes in the selling price. Assume that the selling price is $30 and that the unit variable cost is $20. The selling price is then reduced to $25. This $5 reduction in price has the same effect as a $5 increase in unit variable cost.

Unit basis	Original basis	Increased unit variable cost	Reduced selling price
Selling price	$30	$30	$25
Variable cost	20	25	20
Contribution margin	$10	$ 5	$ 5

The net result will be the same as it was when the variable cost was increased by $5 a unit. In either case, the contribution margin per unit is the same. On a P/V graph, the profit line would be the same as it was in the illustration given in Figure 2-5.

PERCENTAGE CHANGES IN PRICE AND VARIABLE COSTS

A given percentage of reduction in selling price, however, has more effect on profits than the same percentage of increase in variable costs. This is understandable, of course, considering that the original base is greater for the selling price than it is for the variable cost. As a result, the amount of the reduction in selling price is greater. To illustrate, an example is given that compares a 10 percent reduction in the selling price with a 10 percent increase in unit variable cost. Once again assume an original selling price of $30 and a unit variable cost of $20. A 10 percent reduction in the selling price amounts to $3, and a 10 percent increase in the unit variable cost amounts to $2. The effect on the contribution margin is shown below.

	Original basis	10% reduction in selling price	10% increase in unit variable cost
Selling price	$30	$27	$30
Variable cost	20	20	22
Contribution margin	$10	$ 7	$ 8

To maintain the same profits as before, it will be necessary to increase sales volume, and sales volume will have to be increased by a larger amount when the unit contribution margin is lower. In this example, a larger increase in sales volume is required when the selling price is reduced by 10 percent.

OFFSETTING REDUCED CONTRIBUTION MARGINS

A simple equation, a break-even type of equation, can be used to solve for an increase in sales volume that will compensate for a loss in the unit contribution margin. With this additional sales volume, the profits will remain as high as they were before the reduction in the unit contribution margin. There is balance when the contribution margin from the additional units sold is equal to the decrease in contribution margin on the original sales volume.

In the last example, the unit variable cost was increased by $2. An equation is given below that can be used to solve for an increase in sales volume that will make up for a reduction of $2 in the unit contribution margin. Assume that 60,000 units were sold before the change in the contribution margin. The total contribution margin was then $600,000 (60,000 units X $10).

Reduction of $2 per unit in the contribution margin applied to the original 60,000 units sold	=	Contribution margin on additional units to be sold.
$120,000 ($2 X 60,000 units)	=	Contribution margin on additional units to be sold.

The new contribution margin per unit is $8. Therefore, 15,000 additional units must be sold to earn the same profits as before ($120,000 ÷ $8). Stated in another way, sales volume must be increased by 25 percent (15,000/60,000) to make up for a 10 percent increase in unit variable cost.

If desired, the equation can be restated so that the additional units can be solved for directly. A solution is given below for the additional units to be sold to compensate for the 10 percent reduction in selling price.

$$\frac{\text{Reduction of \$3 per unit in the contribution margin applied to the original 60,000 units sold}}{\text{Revised unit contribution margin}} = \text{Additional units to be sold.}$$

$$\frac{\$3 \text{ X } 60,000 \text{ units}}{\$7} = \text{Additional units to be sold.}$$

$$\frac{\$180,000}{\$7} = 25{,}715 \text{ additional units to be sold (approx.).}$$

When the selling price is reduced by 10 percent, sales volume must be increased by 42.9 percent, in the example given, to maintain the same profits as before.

There will be circumstances when an increase in unit variable cost or a reduction in selling price cannot be avoided or may even be desirable. In any case, management will want to know how profits will be affected and how sales volume must be increased to make up for any reduction in unit contribution margin. The equation illustrated above helps to answer these questions.

CHANGES IN FIXED EXPENSES

Profits are also affected by changes in the fixed expenses. Often fixed expenses, if not controlled properly, tend to increase gradually until they reach a point where profits are reduced substantially. A change in the fixed expenses does not change the slope of the profit line. Instead, the profit line shifts to the right or to the left of the original line but remains parallel to the original line. The distance between the revised profit line and the original profit line at any point is equal to the difference in the fixed expenses.

In the illustration given, each unit of product was sold for $30, and the variable cost per unit was $20. The fixed expenses for the year were $300,000. Assume that the fixed expenses can be reduced to $200,000. The new profit line begins at $200,000, and the company can break even with the sale of 20,000 units.

The P/V graph in Figure 2-6 is shown with the new profit line for fixed expenses of $200,000 shown to the left of the original profit line. The distance between the two profit lines is $100,000 at any point.

A COMPARISON OF THREE COMPANIES

It is quite evident that adequate control over both variable and fixed expenses is highly important in successful business operation. A P/V graph can drive this point home better than words. Assume, for example, that there are three companies in a given industry. One is a high-cost producer, another is a medium-cost producer, and the third is a low-cost producer. All three companies sell a certain line of product for $40 a unit. In order to simplify the illustration, it is assumed that the fixed expenses for each of the companies amount to $200,000 a year. The variable costs per unit for each company are given below.

Company A – $20
Company B –   30
Company C –   35

Profit lines for each company are drawn on the P/V graph in Figure 2-7.

P/V Graph

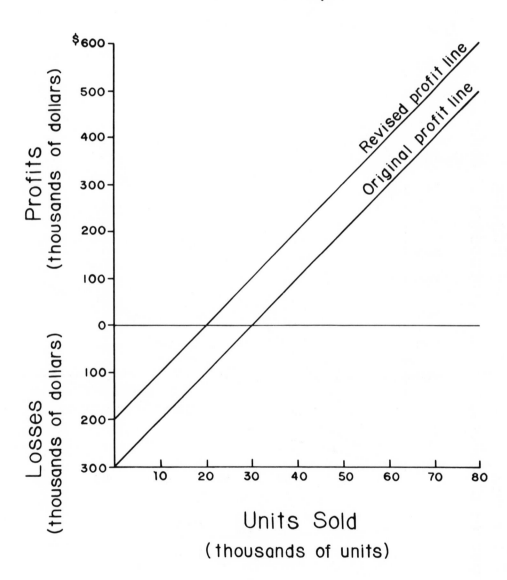

Figure 2-6

P/V Graph

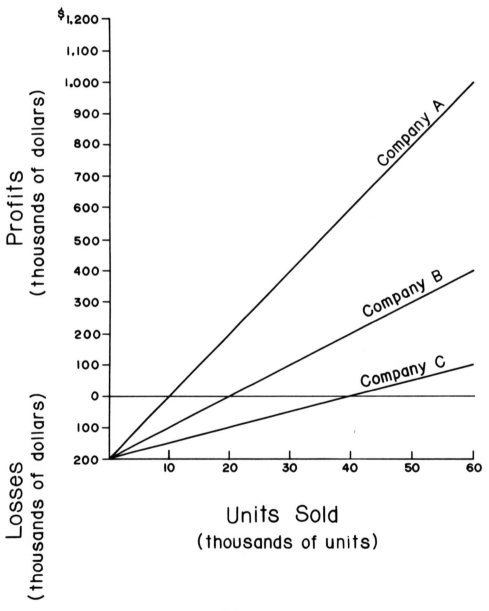

Figure 2-7

Company A has a distinct advantage with low variable costs. It breaks even with the sale of 10,000 units and beyond that point earns a profit of $20 for each additional unit sold. Profits increase at the rate of $200,000 for every 10,000 additional units sold. If the total market for this product should be reduced to a point where each company can sell only 30,000 units, Company A will earn a profit of $400,000 while Company B earns only $100,000 and Company C sustains a loss of $50,000. If prices must be reduced, Company A is in a better position to absorb these reductions. Company C, on the other hand, is in such a poor position that even under present conditions it earns nothing until after 40,000 units are sold. Profits rise slowly at the rate of only $50,000 for each additional 10,000 units sold.

MORE THAN ONE PRODUCT LINE

Up to this point it has been assumed that only one line of product is produced and sold. Ordinarily, there will be several lines of product and even variations of style within each line. Selling prices and the variable costs will be different for each line and, perhaps, for style distinctions within a line.

A break-even chart or a P/V graph can be drawn to represent the total operation, assuming that the product lines are sold in a given proportion. This break-even chart or P/V graph would resemble the ones already illustrated for a single product line.

It is possible, however, to prepare a P/V graph that will show the effect of each line of product on the total operation. The profit line can be drawn with a different slope for each product line according to its contribution margin, and the length of the line for each product will indicate the expected sales volume for that product. Another line can be drawn on the graph to show the combined operation.

A P/V graph with budget estimates for three product lines is given for illustration. Another graph is given for the actual operation, and the results can then be compared with the budget plan. Data with respect to the budget are given below.

Product lines	Estimated sales volume (units)	Selling prices	Unit variable costs	Unit contribution margins	Contribution margin percentages
A	20,000	$20	$10	$10	50%
B	20,000	10	6	4	40
C	10,000	10	8	2	20

Fixed expenses for the year are estimated at $160,000.

The P/V graph for the budget plan is shown in Figure 2-8.

Sales are expressed in dollars of revenue and not in units of product. A total of mixed units has no significance.

Product A, with the highest percentage of contribution margin per unit, is depicted first on the profit line for the individual products. The slope of this segment of the line reveals the rate of profit increase from additional sales of Product A, and the length of the segment measures the total sales revenue expected from this line of product.

P/V Graph
Budget Plan

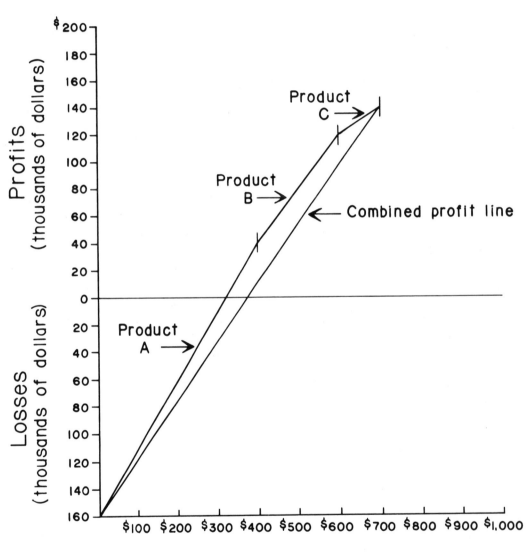

Figure 2-8

Product B contributes proportionately less to profits and is shown next, followed by Product C, which contributes the least proportionately.

The total profit line shows the overall results if the product lines are sold in the predetermined proportions. Note that this line lies to the right of the profit line for the individual products and meets that line only when the total sales budget requirement is fulfilled. It cannot rise at the same rate as the segment of the line represented by Product A because the *average* profit for any revenue level is dampened by the effect of Products B and C. If *only* Product A were sold, for example, the company could break even with revenue of $320,000 ($160,000 fixed expenses ÷ 50% contribution margin percentage). With Products B and C in the sales mix, as stated, the company does not reach break-even point until the mixed revenue is equal to approximately $373,300. This break-even revenue is derived by dividing the fixed expenses by the weighted average contribution margin percentage. The computations are shown below.

Product lines	Sales ratios	Selling prices	Unit contribution margins	*Weighted values Selling prices	Unit contribution margins
A	2	$20	$10	$40	$20
B	2	10	4	20	8
C	1	10	2	10	2
			Totals	$70	$30

*Multiply both selling prices and unit contribution margins by the sales ratios.

The average rate of contribution margin is 42.86% ($30/$70). Or the weighted average contribution margin percentage can be computed from the total data.

$$\frac{\text{Total contribution margin}}{\text{Total sales revenue}} \quad \frac{\$300,000}{\$700,000} \quad = 42.86\%.$$

Break-even revenue for the budgeted sales mix is then $373,300 ($160,000 fixed expenses ÷ .4286 average contribution margin percentage).

The budget plan was not realized as shown on the P/V graph in Figure 2-9 for the actual operation. Although the selling prices and costs were in agreement with the budget estimates and although the overall sales volume was the same as planned, the company did not realize the estimated profit of $140,000 because of shifts in the sales mix. The change in the proportions of products sold is called a *change in the mix*.

During the next year, the three product lines were sold as follows:

Product lines	Number of units sold
A	10,000
B	30,000
C	10,000

P/V Graph
Actual Operation

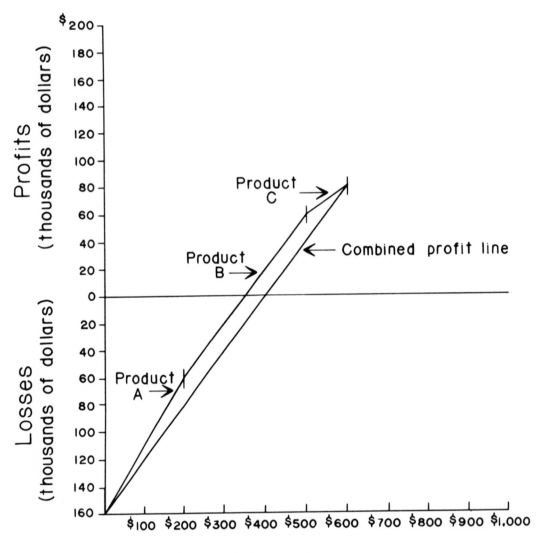

Figure 2-9

With a shift of sales from Product A to Product B, the company earns a profit of $80,000 and not $140,000 as planned. Product B contributes proportionately less to profits than Product A and if sales volume for Product B increases while sales volume for Product A decreases, lower profits can be expected. A computation of the $60,000 decrease in profits is made below.

Product lines	Sales volume Budget	Actual	Sales volume increase (decrease)	Unit contribution margins	Increased (decreased) contribution margin
A	20,000	10,000	(10,000)	$10	($100,000)
B	20,000	30,000	10,000	4	40,000

Net decrease in contribution margin ($ 60,000)

Budgeted profit	$140,000
Less decrease in contribution margin	60,000
Actual profit	$ 80,000

STEPS TOWARD PROFIT IMPROVEMENT

Profits are affected by various factors such as sales volume, selling prices, costs, and the mix of products sold. As a preliminary step in the profit improvement process, actual results can be compared with budget estimates; and visual representations in the form of break-even charts or P/V graphs can often be more helpful than data in a tabulated form.

After the information has been obtained, consideration can be given to steps that may lead to profit improvement. For example, critical problem areas may be identified as shown below, and various corrective measures can be examined.

1. Sales Volume

If sales volume is low, perhaps it can be improved with more vigorous sales promotion. Or certain inducements may have to be offered in the form of additional services to customers. Product lines may not be up to date, and it may be necessary to introduce new or improved products.

2. Price and Cost Structure

Prices may be too high or too low in relation to the prices of the competition. Perhaps, better control is needed over costs. In some cases it may be possible to reduce prices and increase sales volume by more than enough to compensate for the effect of lower prices. If costs can be reduced, the saving in cost or part of it can be passed along to customers by lowering prices. This in turn may increase sales volume and profits.

3. The Sales Mix

Products that yield inadequate contribution margins may be receiving too much attention. Perhaps customers can be induced to switch over to more profitable product lines. Or it may be possible to convert low contribution product lines into high contribution lines by searching for ways to reduce costs or increase prices.

In making any plans, it must be recognized that constraints are imposed by the limitations of existing production facilities and the capacity of the market. Within this framework management can examine various alternatives in an effort to select the best combination.

MODEL BUILDING

In profit planning many questions are likely to arise, questions that are essentially "what if" questions. For example, what will be the effect on profits if the unit variable cost can be reduced by a certain amount? What will happen if prices are reduced in combination with unit variable cost reductions? These questions may be answered by building models and by changing the values of the factors in various combinations. A computer can be programmed to show what will happen under a variety of assumptions. If desired, graphs and charts can also be drawn by the computer to show what can be expected if a given course of action is followed.

SUMMARY

The effect of changes in sales volume, prices, costs, and product mix on profits can be brought out very clearly by graphs or charts. The visual form of presentation, like the view from the top of a mountain, is a panoramic view. An equation showing profits under a certain set of conditions gives a limited picture like the view from the floor of a valley. Both the break-even chart and P/V graph are frequently used in profit planning. The break-even chart shows the slope of both revenue and expense lines while the P/V graph gives the profit or loss effect directly. Visual aids can show what will happen if there are changes in any of the factors that determine profits, and as a result are most useful in profit planning and budgeting.

3

Splitting the
Semivariable Costs

In computing the break-even point, it is essential that costs be identified as accurately as possible as being either variable costs or fixed costs. If a cost is to be controlled properly, it is important to know what the cost will be at a given point and to know how much it changes with variations in some measurable factor such as hours of operation or the number of units processed or sold. This knowledge is also vital in budgeting and in making any plans or decisions. Various alternatives may be available, and management will want accurate cost estimates for each of the various alternatives—cost estimates that can be used to make the correct decision.

COST BEHAVIOR PATTERNS

Some costs can be readily classified as being either fixed or variable costs, but many costs that are designated as semivariable do not fit clearly into either category. The semivariable costs must then be broken down into fixed and variable components, even though the task is somewhat difficult. As already pointed out, the knowledge of how costs will behave under different conditions and under various assumptions is important—so important that management devotes a great deal of time to the study of cost behavior. Certain designated individuals within a company may spend a large part of their time in refining estimates of costs and in searching for better ways to predict cost behavior.

Fixed Costs

Costs of operation may follow certain patterns. A fixed cost, for example, is a cost that does not change as a direct result of changes in hours of operation or as a result of changes in the number of units of product manufactured. On a graph, the fixed costs will appear as a horizontal line. (See Figure 3-1.)

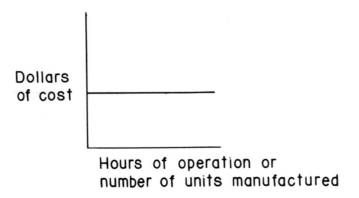

Figure 3-1

Examples of fixed costs are the salary of the plant superintendent, property taxes and insurance, factory rent, and depreciation of plant and equipment. These costs do not increase with increases in hours of operation or with increases in productive output. Fixed costs may be increased or decreased, of course, but the increases or decreases come about as a result of administrative action—that is, someone decides what the cost will be and takes the appropriate action to set the cost at that level. The fixed cost, however, does not go up or down automatically with hours of operation or with the number of units of product produced.

Variable Costs

Variable costs, on the other hand, vary in direct proportion to changes in activity. The variable costs can be depicted on a graph as a straight line that begins at zero and rises according to the rate of variability. (See Figure 3-2.)

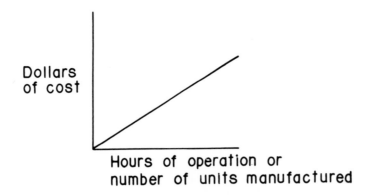

Figure 3-2

An example of variable cost is the cost of the direct materials used to manufacture a product. If only one unit of product is produced, the cost of the direct materials may be $6. If two units of product are produced, the cost will be $12. If three units of product are produced, the cost will be $18. As production increases by one unit, the cost will increase by $6.

Semivariable Costs

A semivariable cost has characteristics that are common to both fixed and variable costs. For example, a plant engineering department may handle repair and maintenance problems. There will be a fixed cost associated with the department, and there may also be costs that vary according to the hours of operation. On a graph this type of cost may be shown as a straight line starting at the point of the fixed cost and sloping upwards as it varies with hours of operation (Figure 3-3), or a cost may begin at a certain point and rise at an increasing or a decreasing rate. That is, the rate of variability is not uniform. (See Figures 3-4 and 3-5.)

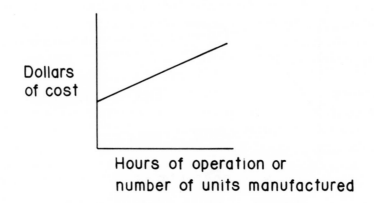

Figure 3-3

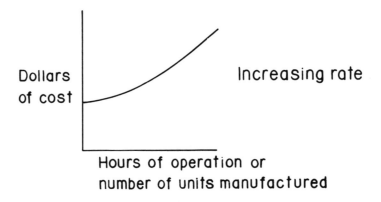

Dollars of cost

Increasing rate

Hours of operation or
number of units manufactured

Figure 3-4

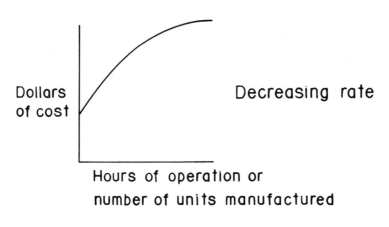

Dollars of cost

Decreasing rate

Hours of operation or
number of units manufactured

Figure 3-5

Sometimes a cost may behave as a fixed cost for a segment of the range and then move up to another level where it remains fixed over another segment of the range before it moves up to still another level. Clerical salaries may fit this pattern. For example, a few employees may be able to handle all of the work up to a certain point, and the salaries will be fixed up at this point. Additional employees may be hired when the work load becomes larger, and the cost will then be fixed at a higher level. This type of cost increases by steps. (See Figure 3-6.)

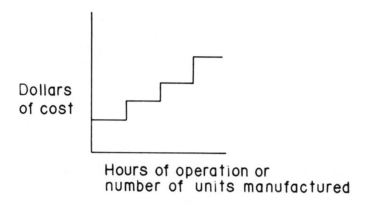

Figure 3-6

COST SEGREGATION TECHNIQUES

Various methods may be used to break costs down into fixed and variable classifications. Often it is not possible to make precise distinctions, but approximations can be made that will represent the average condition. Three methods that are frequently employed for segregating costs into fixed and variable classifications are set forth below.

1. The high and low points method.
2. Fitting a line of average by inspection.
3. Fitting a line of average by equation.

The High and Low Points Method

This method of cost segregation, while not very sophisticated, will give reliable results if the cost varies at a uniform rate over the entire range. The costs and the corresponding hours of activity or other factor used in measurement are listed. The difference between the hours at the highest point of operation and the lowest point is divided into the difference in the costs at these points to arrive at the variable cost per hour. Knowing the variable rate per hour, it is easy to obtain the total variable cost for any number of hours and subtract the result from the total cost to obtain the fixed cost.

An example is given for maintenance cost, assumed for the purpose of this example to be a semivariable cost. Hours and costs are listed from past records for various activity levels.

Hours of operation	*Maintenance cost*
130,000	$286,000
110,000	246,000
140,000	306,000
90,000	206,000
160,000	346,000
175,000	376,000
120,000	266,000
180,000	386,000
150,000	326,000
190,000	406,000

Hours range from a low of 90,000 hours to a high of 190,000 hours, and costs from a low of $206,000 to a high of $406,000.

	Hours	*Cost*
High	190,000	$406,000
Low	90,000	206,000
Difference	100,000	$200,000

$$\frac{\$200,000 \quad \text{cost difference}}{100,000 \quad \text{hour difference}} = \begin{array}{l}\$2 \text{ an hour, rate of}\\ \text{cost variability.}\end{array}$$

Maintenance cost varies at the rate of $2 per hour, and the fixed cost can be computed at any point. For example, at 120,000 hours the variable cost will be $240,000 (120,000 hours x $2 variable rate), and this amount is subtracted from the total cost of $266,000 at this level to obtain a fixed cost of $26,000. If the cost varies at a uniform rate, the fixed cost can be determined at any point. At 150,000 hours, for example, the variable cost will be $300,000. The variable cost of $300,000 is subtracted from the total cost of $326,000 leaving $26,000 as the fixed cost.

In the illustration given, the variable portion of the cost varied at a uniform rate over the entire range. This will not always be the case. The cost may vary at a constant rate for a portion of the range, but the rate of variability may change as the hours increase. A careful examination of cost behavior at different points will reveal how the cost changes with respect to hours.

Fitting a Line of Regression by Inspection

The high and low points method has the advantage of simplicity, but it may not always be realistic. For any given number of hours it is assumed that there is a certain cost. This will not always be true. The cost will not always be *exactly* the same for any given number of hours, but will probably be somewhat different even though the company operates for the same number of hours as measured at different times during the course of its operation. However, the cost for a given number of hours will most likely fall with a range, and an average cost can be determined.

Costs obtained from historical records for various hours of operation can be plotted on a scattergram with the Y or vertical axis representing costs and the X or horizontal axis representing hours of activity. However, care must be taken in using data drawn from historical records. Abnormal conditions of operation may distort the results, or some peculiarity in the accounting method may cause differences. All abnormal data should be eliminated or adjusted in the process of segregating costs.

A line of average can be drawn through the properly plotted data by visual inspection. This line is called a line of regression when fitted to data that vary with changes in some other variable.

The average known as an arithmetic mean, it will be recalled, is a balancing point. The sum of the variations of the data above this point is equal to the sum of the variations of the data below this point. The balancing point where the algebraic sum of the deviations is equal to zero is the average or arithmetic mean. A line of regression is a line drawn so that the sum of the distances of all points above the line is equal to the sum of the distances of all points below the line.

A cost scattergram is given in Figure 3-7, and a line of regression is fitted to the data.

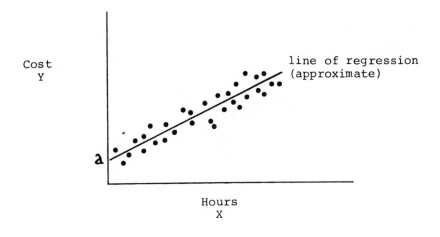

Figure 3-7

Each point on the scattergram represents an historical cost measured at a certain number of hours of operation. In the example it can be seen that these points fall into a pattern, and a line of regression can be drawn to represent the cost pattern. The fixed cost designated as "a" is the level of cost for zero hours of operation; the variable cost is the slope of the line—in other words, the change in cost with respect to the change in hours.

Sometimes it will be quite easy to fit an approximate line of regression to the data by inspection. This line is a rough approximation at best; if more refinement is desired, a line of regression can be solved for by equation.

Fitting a Line of Regression by Equation

The equation for any straight line is given below.

$$Y = a + bX.$$

This equation is a concise way of saying that the line begins at point *a,* and that any point on the vertical scale *Y* is equal to the point *a* plus a given proportion of a horizontal measurement X. The proportion of X designated as *b* defines the slope of the line. An example is given in Figure 3-8.

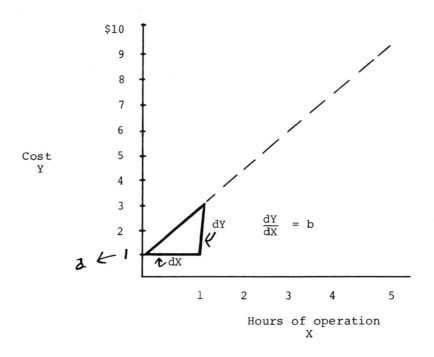

Figure 3-8

The line begins at point *a* and rises at a rate defined by $\frac{dY}{dX}$, or in other words, *b.*

dY = difference in Y.

dX = difference in X.

The line can be continued as indicated by the dotted line by adding the porportion of the value of X to the fixed cost *a.*

The equation for this example is:

$$Y = a + bX$$
$$\text{or}$$
$$Y = 1 + 2X.$$

The fixed cost is $1 and Y increases by 2 for every change of 1 in X. The values of Y for various values of X are given below.

X	Y
2	5
3	7
4	9

If a line of regression is to be drawn to represent many cost measurements, the equation can be given as follows:

$$\Sigma Y = na + b\Sigma X.$$

The sum of the Y values is equal to the number of fixed points (n x a) plus the proportion b multiplied by the sum of the X values.

Solve for the fixed cost (a) and the variable rate (b) by simultaneous equations. Multiply all terms by X to obtain another equation.

$$\Sigma XY = \Sigma Xa + b\Sigma X^2 .$$

Use numerical values for X and Y and solve for a and b.

$$\Sigma Y = na + b\Sigma X$$
$$\Sigma XY = \Sigma Xa + b\Sigma X^2 .$$

The value for a becomes the fixed cost, and the value for b becomes the variable rate. The line can then be fitted to the data.

An example is given based on historical cost data for various hours of operation. In order to simplify the arithmetic computations, only 12 items of data are used with unrealistically small dollar amounts. In practice, more items of data would be used and both the number of hours and the costs would probably be much higher.

Historical Data

Hours of operation	*Cost*
5	$ 9
10	12
15	18
20	29
25	28
30	25
35	38
40	38
45	50
50	53
55	65
60	61

*The company may also operate the same number of hours over different time periods with slight variations in cost. For example, at one time with 60 hours of operation the cost may be $60. At some other time for 60 hours, the cost may be $62. All cost data including data for repetitions of the same hourly levels would be included in an actual situation.

Numerical values can now be computed and assigned to n, ΣX, ΣY, ΣXY, and ΣX^2 in the equations.

$n = 12$ (number of items of data).

Hours of operation X	*Cost* Y	XY	X^2
5	9	45	25
10	12	120	100
15	18	270	225
20	29	580	400
25	28	700	625
30	25	750	900
35	38	1,330	1,225
40	38	1,520	1,600
45	50	2,250	2,025
50	53	2,650	2,500
55	65	3,575	3,025
60	61	3,660	3,600
$\Sigma X = $ 390	$\Sigma Y = $ 426	$\Sigma XY = $ 17,450	$\Sigma X^2 = $ 16,250

The simultaneous equations are given again, and values are substituted for the letters.

$$(1) \quad \Sigma Y = na + b \Sigma X$$
$$(2) \quad \Sigma XY = \Sigma Xa + b \Sigma X^2$$
$$(1) \quad 426 = 12a + 390b$$
$$(2) \quad 17,450 = 390a + 16,250b$$

Multiply equation (1) by 390 and equation (2) by 12 to eliminate *a*.

$$(1) \quad 166,140 = 4,680a + 152,100b$$
$$(2) \quad 209,400 = 4,680a + 195,000b$$
$$42,900b = 43,260$$
$$b = \$1.00 \text{ (approx.)}$$

The cost varies at an average rate of $1.00 per hour. Solve for the fixed cost, *b*.

$$426 = 12a + (390 \times \$1.00)$$
$$426 = 12a + 390$$
$$12a = 36$$
$$a = \$3.00.$$

The costs for the various hours are plotted on the graph in Figure 3-9. The line of regression is drawn starting at the fixed costs of $3, and the line rises at the rate of $1 per hour.

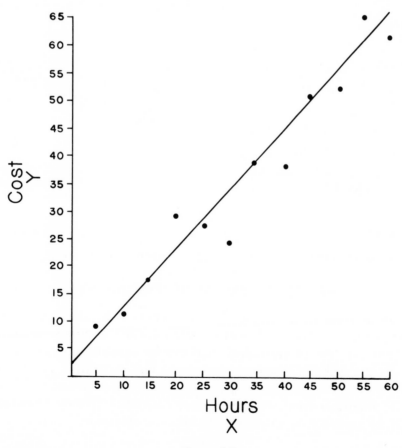

Figure 3-9

CORRELATION

A line of regression may be drawn from visual inspection or from equations, but the line of regression may or may not be significant. If a cost tends to vary with hours of activity or with changes in some other measurable factor, it will be possible to estimate the cost under various conditions with reasonable accuracy. On the other hand, if a cost varies in a random fashion with no apparent relationship between the cost and the hours or other factor selected, there is no basis for predicting what the cost is likely to be at any point. As stated earlier, it must be remembered that the data cannot be plotted blindly but must be examined first to determine whether or not peculiarities in accounting or some other abnormalities of operation have caused the variation.

On the graph in Figure 3-10, there is no discernible relationship between the cost and the hours of operation. The cost is distributed randomly and does not seem to increase or decrease with increases in hours of operation.

The graph in Figure 3-11, however, shows a definite tendency for costs to vary with hours of operation. When a variable such as a cost tends to vary in relation to changes in another variable, there is *correlation*. In the graph given below, it is quite evident that the cost data follow a pattern and that there is a high degree of correlation between the hours and the cost.

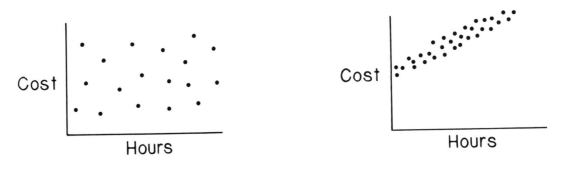

Figure 3-10   Figure 3-11

The costs increase with increases in hours and almost form a line on the graph.

THE COEFFICIENT OF DETERMINATION

The degree of correlation can be measured by what is called the coefficient of determination or the r^2. The coefficient of determination measures the percentage of variations from the line of regression that can be explained by changes in some measurable factor such as hours of operation. The correlation is very good, for example, if 90 percent of the variations can be attributed to variations in hours of operation. On the other hand, there is a poor correlation if only 15 percent of the variations can be explained by changes in the hours of operation.

The measurement of correlation depends upon a relationship between standard deviations. The concept of a standard deviation is often used in making statistical measurements. The standard deviation is equal to the square root of the sum of the squares of the deviations from the mean divided by the number of items and is designated by the Greek letter sigma (σ). This can be expressed by equation with N representing the number of items, X representing the deviation, and $\overline{X}$ representing the mean (arithmetic mean).

$$\sigma = \sqrt{\frac{(X - \overline{X})^2}{N}}$$

standard
deviation

In the normal distribution of data, approximately 2/3 of the data (more precisely 68.27%) lie within the range of plus and minus one standard deviation from the mean (average). Assume that data have been plotted in a frequency distribution as shown by the curve given in Figure 3-12.

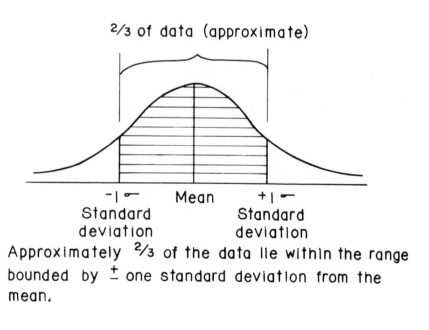

Figure 3-12

This concept of statistical measurement can also be applied in the measurement of the dispersion of costs around the mean. On Graph I (Figure 3-13) an average cost has been computed, and lines have been drawn to set boundaries for the standard deviation.

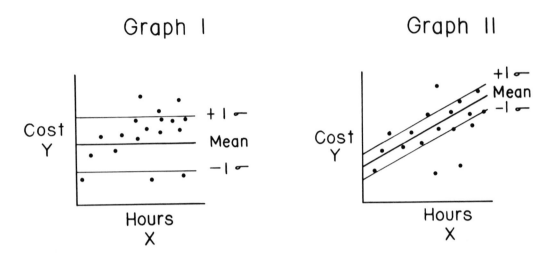

Figure 3-13   **Figure 3-14**

A line of regression with the average influenced by the hours of operation can also be drawn on a graph and bounded by lines at a distance of ± one standard deviation from the mean.

The percentage of the variation from the mean as shown on Graph II (Figure 3-14) to the variation from the mean as shown on Graph I is the percentage of the total variations that cannot be explained by changes in the hours of operation. Subtract this percentage from one (100%) to obtain the percentage of changes that can be explained by changes in the hours. This final percentage is the r^2 or the coefficient of determination that measures the degree of correlation between the cost and the hours of operation. The equation is given below.

$$r^2 = 1 - \frac{\sigma^2 \quad \text{(Graph II)}}{\sigma^2 \quad \text{(Graph I)}}$$

or

$$r^2 = 1 - \frac{\text{square of the standard deviation on Graph II}}{\text{square of the standard deviation on Graph I}}$$

or

$$r^2 = 1 - \frac{\text{Variations not explained by changes in X}}{\text{Total variations.}}$$

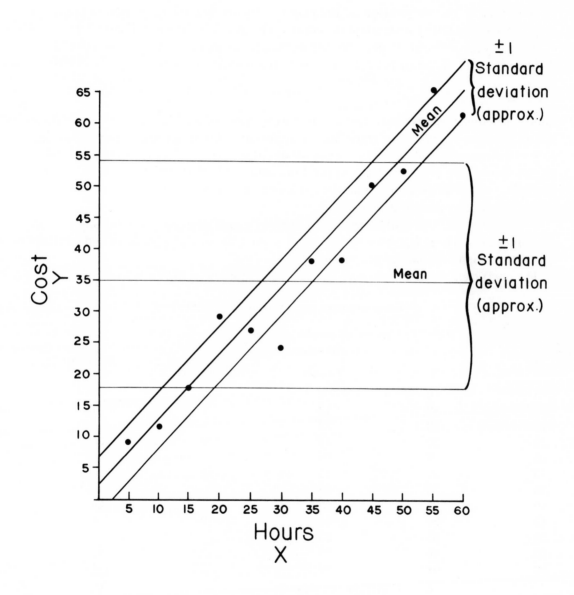

Figure 3-15

Obviously, r^2 will be large and the correlation will be good if the standard deviation measured from the line of regression on Graph II is relatively small compared with the standard deviation for the total data as measured on Graph I.

An Example of Correlation

Data used in the preparation of the graph in Figure 3-9 are again used to prepare a graph that shows lines for standard deviations. This graph is shown in Figure 3-15.

The average without respect to the influence of hours has been computed by dividing the sum of the costs (ΣY) of 426 by the number of items, 12.

$$\frac{426}{12} \quad = \quad \$35 \text{ average cost (approx.)}$$

Limiting boundaries have been formed by drawing lines of standard deviation on either side of the lines of average or regression by approximation. If approximately 2/3 of the data fits within plus and minus one standard deviation, then 1/3 of the data lies outside of this limit with 1/6 above the upper limit and 1/6 below the lower limit. In this example, two items (1/6 of 12) lie above plus one standard deviation and two items lie below minus one standard deviation.

From the graph, it is quite evident that there is a high degree of correlation between cost and hours. There is a very narrow band around the line of regression and a rather wide band around the line of general average.

The coefficient of determination or r^2 can be computed as shown below.

Deviations from the Line of Regression Squared

X	Y	Line of regression, Y values	Deviations	Deviations squared
5	9	8	1	1
10	12	13	1	1
15	18	18	—	—
20	29	23	6	36
25	28	28	—	—
30	25	33	8	64
35	38	38	—	—
40	38	43	5	25
45	50	48	2	4
50	53	53	—	—
55	65	58	7	49
60	61	63	2	4
		Sum of deviations squared		184

Divide the sum of the deviations squared by N (by 12 in this example).

$$\frac{184}{12} = 15.33 \text{ standard deviation squared .}$$

**Deviations from the
Line of General Average Squared**

X	Y	Average Y	Deviation	Deviations squared
5	9	35	26	676
10	12	35	23	529
15	18	35	17	289
20	29	35	6	36
25	28	35	7	49
30	25	35	10	100
35	38	35	3	9
40	38	35	3	9
45	50	35	15	225
50	53	35	18	324
55	65	35	30	900
60	61	35	26	676

Sum of deviations squared $\underline{\underline{3,822}}$

Divide the sum of the deviations
squared by N (by 12 in this example).

$$\frac{3,822}{12} = 318.5 \text{ standard deviation squared.}$$

$$r^2 = 1 - \frac{15.33}{318.5}$$

$$r^2 = 95.2\%$$

The r^2, as computed above, is equal to one minus the result of dividing the standard deviation around the line of regression squared by the standard deviation around the line of general average squared.

With r^2 at 95.2 percent, it is much easier to predict cost for a given number of hours and have assurance that the actual cost should be relatively close to the estimate.

THE SIGNIFICANCE OF CORRELATION STUDIES

A great deal of effort is made by many companies in searching for measurable factors to which cost behavior can be related. Correlation studies are made to find out if a given cost does tend to vary with the quantity of materials used, labor hours, machine hours, sales of related products, and other measurable factors that may be available. It is not necessary to prove a cause and effect relationship. The important point is to show that the cost tends to vary by a certain amount when a measurable factor increases or decreases by a certain amount.

If it is found that a particular cost does go up or down with the changes in some other variable and if there is a high degree of correlation, then the company has the means for estimating that cost with greater precision. This rigorous approach to the study of cost behavior makes it possible to control costs more closely and to prepare more accurate budget plans. Furthermore, costs used for break-even analysis in various profit planning situations and for decision-making purposes will be more reliable.

SUMMARY

It is not easy to classify costs precisely as variable costs or as fixed costs. Yet this distinction must be made as accurately as possible if costs are to be controlled, budgeted, and used in decision making.

An approximate analysis of costs by behavior characteristics can be made by the high and low points method. In most cases, however, a more refined method will be required. Costs for various hours of activity or for various number of units produced can be plotted on a graph. A line of regression can be fitted to the data either by visual inspection or by equation. The line begins at the fixed costs and rises at a rate that can be defined as the rate of variability per hour or per unit of product.

In relating cost variability to some measurable factor, it is necessary to determine that the cost does in fact change with changes in the factor. Is there valid correlation? If it can be demonstrated that there is a high degree of correlation between the cost and the factor selected, then management has a better basis for the estimation of costs. This in turn can lead to improved profitability.

4

Combining the Advantages of Variable Costing and Absorption Costing

In cost accounting, the costs of manufacturing the products are assigned to the products and are traced through the accounting records as a part of their cost. There is some difference of opinion with respect to which manufacturing costs should be attached to the products. According to one theory that is frequently employed in practice, *all* costs of manufacturing are product costs—both the fixed and the variable costs. When all of the manufacturing costs are treated as product costs, the company is costing products by the *absorption costing* method.

Another method of costing products, frequently referred to as either *direct costing* or *variable costing,* identifies only the variable manufacturing costs with the products. The fixed costs of manufacturing do not become a part of product cost but are instead charged off as expenses of operation during the fiscal period. Although this method is often designated as direct costing, it is more accurate to call it variable costing. The variable manufacturing costs are assigned to the products. Some costs may be direct costs inasmuch as they are directly related to a certain product line, but they may also be fixed costs, in which case they do not become product cost according to this method of costing. In this book, the method of costing that assigns only the variable manufacturing costs to the products will be referred to as the variable costing method.

Each costing method has its own peculiar advantages, and in practice a company will not follow one method so exclusively that it overlooks the advantages of the other. For example, absorption costing may be used for reporting profits and costing inventories while at the same time statistical data are developed on a variable costing basis to furnish management with information on the contribution margins from the various product lines. Conversely, a company that traces costs through its accounting records on a variable costing basis will prepare special reports showing product line profits after fixed costs have been deducted. In addition, the company using variable costing will be as concerned with the utilization of productive capacity and the absorption of fixed costs as the company using absorption costing. The distinction between the two methods, as they are employed in practice, is fundamentally based upon the way in which inventory costs are determined as a part of the income measurement process.

ASSIGNING COSTS TO THE PRODUCTS

The two costing methods can be compared briefly as shown below.

1. Absorption costing — *All the costs of manufacturing* are to be assigned to the products, both the fixed and variable costs.
2. Variable costing — *Only the variable costs of manufacturing* are product costs. The fixed manufacturing costs are period costs. They are charged to the fiscal period as expense and are not carried as a part of the product cost.

Absorption Costing

The fixed manufacturing costs are often somewhat difficult to identify with the products. A large part of the difficulty arises because of the nature of the fixed costs. Fixed costs by definition remain the same whether one unit of product is manufactured or many units of product are manufactured. As a result, the fixed cost for each unit of product manufactured depends upon how many units are manufactured during the fiscal period. For example, if the fixed cost is $100,000 and only one unit of product is produced, the fixed cost per unit is $100,000. If 100,000 units are produced, the fixed cost per unit is $1.

The costs of the direct materials and direct labor used in manufacturing products are usually variable with respect to the number of units produced, and can ordinarily be identified with the products by measuring the quantity of material and labor used to make the products and by assigning costs to the measured quantities. Other manufacturing costs are not as directly related to the products and create problems in cost accounting. These other manufacturing costs are various, consisting of factory supplies used, factory supervisory salaries, heat and light, repairs and maintenance, insurance, property taxes, depreciation, and any other costs of manufacturing aside from the cost of the direct materials incorporated in the product and the cost of direct labor used to produce it. Collectively, these other manufacturing costs are called the manufacturing overhead costs.

Ordinarily, the manufacturing overhead costing problem is resolved by agreeing upon a normal or average level of production for a fiscal year. During the fiscal year, the fixed manufacturing-overhead costs (as well as the variable manufacturing overhead costs) are assigned to the products by a predetermined rate computed by dividing the budgeted costs by the normal hours of operation. Any difference between the costs assigned to the products by this rate and the actual costs is treated as a variation to be charged or credited to operations.

A normal level of operating capacity is difficult to define precisely. In general, it represents an average utilization of the plant over the long run. Variations from year to year are expected, with the normal level of operation being an average over the years of a business cycle. It would be unrealistic to state that either the theoretical or practical plant capacity represents a normal level of operation. Often a normal level is a compromise between practical plant capacity over the years and the demand in the market.

Returning to the last example, assume that normal production has been established at 50,000 units of product a year. Each unit of product will be assigned $2 of the fixed manufacturing cost of $100,000. If only 49,000 units are manufactured during the year, the products will bear $98,000 of the fixed cost (49,000 units x $2). The remaining fixed cost of $2,000 that has not been absorbed by the products is then written off to operations as expense—as a variation; specifically, an idle capacity variance.

Variable Costing

Variable costing operates on the theory that the fixed manufacturing cost is in reality not the cost of making products but is an annual cost to have the *capability* of making products. In a sense, the fixed cost is an annual membership fee permitting the company to operate as a manufacturer. Only the costs that vary with production are considered to be costs of the products.

In variable costing there is no problem of deciding how the fixed costs should be allocated to the products. Instead, there is the problem of making a clear-cut distinction between variable costs and fixed costs. This only emphasizes the importance of separating the semivariable costs into their variable and fixed components.

A theoretical discussion in support of either method lies beyond the scope of this book. Each method is helpful when used properly, and there are benefits to be derived in combining the advantages from both methods. Those who favor absorption costing as a more logical basis for product costing still must use the principles of variable costing in controlling costs and in making plans for the future. And those who favor variable costing must still consider the problems of idle plant capacity and the ways in which the plant capacity can be used to the best advantage.

A COMPARATIVE ILLUSTRATION

Income statements using the same cost and revenue data for a year are given to illustrate the differences between the two costing methods. Assume that the plant can produce 80,000 units of product when operating at normal capacity. There is no inventory at the beginning of the year, 60,000 units of product are manufactured during the year, and 50,000 units are sold. Revenue and cost data are given below.

Unit selling price	$ 15
Unit variable manufacturing cost	9
Unit variable selling and administrative expense	1
Fixed manufacturing cost	120,000
Fixed selling and administrative expense	50,000

With a variable costing system, only the variable manufacturing cost of $9 per unit is assigned to the products. All of the other costs are charged to expense during the fiscal period.

With an absorption costing system, the fixed manufacturing cost is allocated to the products. The amount of fixed cost to be assigned to each unit is determined at the normal capacity level of 80,000 units. This rate will be used even if it is known in advance that production will not be up to this level. The products should bear the cost of a normal operation, and a separate measurement should be made of any variation as information that can be helpful in guiding future operations. The variations from a normal operation should not be hidden in the product costs. The fixed manufacturing cost per unit of product in this example is $1.50 ($120,000 ÷ 80,000 units). The total unit product cost is $10.50, the unit variable manufacturing cost of $9 plus the unit fixed manufacturing cost of $1.50.

Income statements for the year appear below.

	Variable Costing	Absorption Costing
Sales (50,000 units @ $15)	$750,000	$750,000
Cost of goods sold:		
Cost of goods produced:		
Variable manufacturing cost (60,000 x $9)	$540,000	$540,000
Fixed manufacturing cost (60,000 x $1.50)	–	90,000
Total cost of goods produced	$540,000	$630,000
Less inventory at end of year:		
Variable cost (10,000 x $9)	90,000	
Variable and fixed cost (10,000 x $10.50)		105,000
Cost of goods sold	$450,000	$525,000
Contribution margin, manufacturing	$300,000	
Gross profit	–	$225,000
Variable selling and administrative expenses (50,000 x $1.00)	50,000	$ 50,000
Contribution margin (final)	$250,000	–
Fixed manufacturing costs	$120,000	–
Capacity variance	–	30,000
Fixed selling and administrative costs	50,000	50,000
Total	$170,000	$130,000
Net income before income taxes	$ 80,000	$ 95,000
Income taxes, 50 percent	40,000	47,500
Net income after income taxes	$ 40,000	$ 47,500

The variable costing statement closely follows the concepts used in break-even analysis, with the variable costs and the fixed costs separated. The variable costs are subtracted from sales revenue, leaving a final contribution margin of $250,000 that is equal to one-third of sales revenue. The fixed costs are then subtracted to obtain the net income. On this statement it is easier to see how the volume of sales affects profits. For example, with fixed costs of $170,000 and a contribution margin of 33-1/3 percent, it is a simple matter to compute the break-even point.

$$\frac{\$170,000 \quad \text{fixed costs}}{.333 \quad \text{contribution margin percentage}} = \$510,000 \text{ revenue at break-even point}$$

Or what will the profit be before income taxes if the plant operates at a normal capacity of 80,000 units and sells the entire output.

Unit selling	$15
Unit variable cost (total)	10
Unit contribution margin	$ 5

80,000 units sold x $5 unit contribution margin = $400,000 total contribution margin.

Total contribution margin	$400,000
Less total fixed costs	170,000
Net income before income taxes	$230,000

The variable and fixed manufacturing costs are mingled together on the absorption costing statement as product cost, and the contribution margin is not revealed. This statement, however, unlike the variable costing statement, does show that the productive facilities were not used as intended. Profits do not depend upon sales alone. Productive facilities must be used properly, and this statement is more informative in that respect. The capacity variance is a measurement of the portion of the fixed manufacturing cost that was not assigned to the products because production was below the normal level. The fixed manufacturing cost of $1.50 a unit was computed on the basis of a normal production of 80,000 units. Actually only 60,000 units were produced, with the result that only $90,000 of the fixed manufacturing costs of $120,000 were applied to the products. The remaining $30,000 that was not absorbed by the products is charged off during the year as a capacity variance. From an accounting and income tax point of view, an unabsorbed capacity variance may be of such magnitude that it will have a material effect on profits and income taxes, in which case it may not be advisable to charge it off in one year.

Note that the net income before income taxes is $15,000 higher on the absorption costing statement. This difference of $15,000 results from holding fixed manufacturing costs of $15,000 in the final inventory according to absorption costing principles. There are 10,000 units in the inventory with a fixed manufacturing cost of $1.50 per unit or a total fixed manufacturing cost of $15,000. This cost is not matched against revenue as expense and won't be matched against revenue until the inventory is sold.

On the variable costing statement, none of the fixed manufacturing cost is held over as a part of the inventory cost. All of the fixed manufacturing cost is charged off as expense.

Many companies that use variable costing for planning and control convert to absorption costing at the end of the year to meet the requirements of income tax law and the generally accepted requirements of financial reporting. Also companies using variable costing may believe that reporting on capacity utilization statistically is more meaningful than reporting on the under or over absorption of fixed costs.

THE WEAKNESSES OF EACH COSTING METHOD

Each method of costing has its own peculiar advantages and weaknesses. As already stated, the variable costing method makes a sharp distinction between variable and fixed costs and follows the general concepts employed in break-even analysis. This makes it easier to estimate profits, given certain assumptions with respect to sales volume, sales mix, prices, and costs. The absorption costing method does not offer this advantage, but it does reveal whether or not the productive facilities are being used as intended.

An operation may become unbalanced if too much emphasis is placed on the concepts of variable costing. Short-run advantages may be accepted with little or no thought being given to the long-run consequences. For example, there may be a temptation to reduce prices in order to obtain increased sales volume and increased profits. Or new product lines may be accepted that contribute little to the total operation. Sales volume may increase and profits may also increase. Apparently, this is what is desired and the policy has been successful. But has it been successful, or has it been as successful as it could be? The volume of business may be high, but the facilities and resources are perhaps not being used to the best advantage. With less strain, it may be possible to have even better profits and profits that will be more secure over the long run. A policy that is successful on a short-run basis may prove to be troublesome in later years.

It is also possible to have unbalance when too much attention is paid to the information derived from an absorption costing system. With fixed manufacturing costs included as a part of product cost, the cost per unit will obviously be higher than it would be if only the variable costs were included. With the higher unit cost, management may be reluctant to reduce prices even when such reductions would be desirable. It may seem that to reduce a price below full cost will bring about losses. There is a tendency to forget that fixed costs have been allocated over the products and that these costs will not increase as more units of product are manufactured. Only the variable costs increase in total as more units are manufactured. Therefore, if a product is sold at a price in excess of *variable* cost, there is a contribution to the recovery of fixed costs and to profits. The total contribution margin increases with increases in sales volume.

The idle capacity problem may be aggravated if prices are not reduced under appropriate circumstances. It may also be aggravated if new product lines are rejected because they cannot be sold at prices in excess of *total* unit costs even though the prices are above the unit variable costs.

SEEKING A BALANCED STRATEGY

Ideally there should be balance between the short-run contribution margin and the long-run use of productive facilities. There are no easy answers, but certain approaches to the problem can be helpful. Sometimes limitations will be imposed by the market situation or by peculiarities of the product, and these handicaps may be hard to overcome. Even so, an examination of the problem may reveal conditions that can be improved.

If there is a problem of unused plant capacity, it will be necessary to search for ways to use this capacity to the best advantage. In some cases, the solution may be to increase the sales volume of existing product lines or to introduce new product lines. Perhaps an investigation should be made to determine whether or not idle capacity can be absorbed by manufacturing parts or components that are presently being purchased from outside suppliers for use in production.

The contribution margin per unit of product, while very important, may not be the most important consideration. A limitation is imposed by the productive facilities, and these facilities must be used to earn the best possible profits. Therefore, it may be more appropriate to determine the contribution margin per hour of available capacity and to look upon this amount as a balancing point in making decisions.

Assume, for example, that a company earns a satisfactory total contribution margin from the facilities employed and that there is idle capacity available. The fixed manufacturing costs not absorbed by operations, in other words the capacity variance, amount to $150,000. There are 50,000 hours that are available for additional production. These hours should, of course, be employed to earn the best possible contribution margin. As a starting point in the planning operation, a contribution margin per hour can be computed.

$$\text{Contribution margin from 50,000 hours} = \text{Capacity variance of } \$150,000$$

$$\text{Contribution margin per hour} = \frac{\text{Capacity variance of } \$150,000}{\text{Hours available,} \quad 50,000}$$

Contribution margin per hour $-$ $3.00

Without considering the limitation of hours, the company may become interested in a product line (Product #1) that sells for $20 a unit with unit variable costs of $10. The 50 percent contribution margin appears to be quite attractive, inasmuch as half of the revenue from product sales can be applied to the recovery of fixed costs and to profits. Product #1 seems to be more acceptable than another product line (Product #2), selling for $18 a unit with unit variable costs of $12. Contribution margins are compared below on a unit-of-product basis.

| | Product lines | |
	1	2
Selling price	$20	$18
Unit variable cost	10	12
Unit contribution margin	10	6
Contribution margin percentage	50%	33-1/3%

When the two product lines are compared on the basis of the time required for their production it is found that one hour is required to produce a unit of product #1 while 2 units of product #2 can be produced in an hour. On a time basis, product #2 can yield better profits.

| | Product Lines | |
	1	2
Contribution margin (per unit of product)	$10	$ 6
Contribution margin (per hour)	10	12

With 50,000 hours available, it is possible to produce either 50,000 units of Product #1 or 100,000 units of Product #2. The total contribution margin from the sale of 50,000 units of Product #1 is $500,000. If the 50,000 hours are used to produce 100,000 units of Product #2, the total contribution margin from the sale of these units amounts to $600,000. Unless there are other constraints or other more attractive alternatives available, the company should use the additional capacity for the production of Product #2.

STEPS TOWARD PROFIT OPTIMIZATION

The principle applied in searching for ways to use idle productive capacity can also be applied in planning the total operation. The minimum contribution margin per hour to break even can be computed at the normal level of operations and can serve as a sort of break-even guide to rate the various product lines. The contribution margin per hour that is required to absorb the fixed manufacturing cost at a normal level of operations is also the rate used to apply fixed manufacturing cost to the products, assuming that the costs are applied on the basis of hours.

For example, assume that fixed manufacturing costs amount to $800,000 a year and that the company operates 200,000 hours at normal capacity. In order to break even, an average contribution margin of $4 an hour is required. With a time constraint of 200,000 hours, attention should be directed to increasing the sales of product lines contributing more than $4 an hour and to reducing the sales of product lines contributing less than $4 an hour. Before making any final judgment, however, the long-run prospects should be examined. Perhaps weaker product lines must be kept in order to obtain sales for the stronger lines. The contribution margin per hour is only one criterion that must be considered along with others in rating a product line.

In the illustration given below it is assumed that four product lines that utilize 200,000 hours of capacity are produced and sold as indicated.

Product lines	Contribution margin per unit of product	Production hours per unit of product	Contribution margin per hour	Number of hours	Total Contribution margin
1	$12	3	$4	60,000	$ 240,000
2	10	2	5	80,000	400,000
3	8	1	8	50,000	400,000
4	3	1/2	6	10,000	60,000
			Totals	200,000	$1,100,000

The average contribution margin per hour is $5.50.

$$\frac{\$1,100,000}{200,000 \text{ hours}} \quad \text{total contribution margin} = \$5.50.$$

Although Product #1 yields the highest contribution margin on a unit-of-product basis, it yields only the minimum contribution margin per hour, assuming fixed manufacturing costs of $800,000. Product #2 is somewhat below the average with a contribution of $5 a unit. The total contribution margin can be improved if the time spent in manufacturing Products #1 and #2 can be shifted over to the production of Products #3 and #4.

Profits are maximized by using productive time to the best advantage. An optimum profit solution can be derived by using the technique of *linear programming*. A discussion of linear programming, however, lies beyond the scope of this book. Essentially it is a semi-algebraic approach to the problem of determining the best combination of product lines in the sales mix, and several good books on this subject are available.*

SUMMARY

A system of cost accounting that attempts to assign all of the manufacturing costs to the products is designated as an *absorption cost accounting system*. If only the variable manufacturing costs are to be assigned to the products, costs are being assigned by a *variable costing system* (direct costing system). Each method of costing has its advantages and its disadvantages. With absorption costing it is difficult to determine the contribution margin inasmuch as there is no distinction made between variable costs and fixed costs. On the other hand, an absorption costing system shows whether or not the productive facilities are being used properly. Variable costing follows the

---

*The basic elements of linear programming are discussed briefly in Vajda, S., *An Introduction to Linear Programming and The Theory of Games,* John Wiley & Sons, Inc., New York, 1960, and in Stockton, R. Stansbury, *Introduction to Linear Programming,* Allyn and Bacon, Inc., Boston, 1960. A more complete treatment is presented in Loomba, N. Paul, *Linear Programming,* McGraw-Hill Book Company, New York, 1964.

break-even concept closely and stresses the contribution margin, but it does not show whether or not the facilities are being used properly.

The two methods when used together can help to bring about a balanced operation. The idle capacity variance when divided by the available hours yields an average contribution margin per hour that should be obtained from products sold to absorb the idle capacity. Product lines may also be rated by the contribution margin per hour, comparing the contribution margin per hour for each product with the average contribution margin per hour required to absorb the fixed manufacturing costs. A limitation is imposed by the relative scarcity of productive facilities, and the contribution margin per hour may prove to be as valuable in planning, if not more valuable, than the contribution margin per unit of product.

5

Improving Profits
by Better Cost Control

If costs can be controlled more effectively, a company will obviously earn larger profits— everything else being equal. Inasmuch as costs are an important determinant of profit, it is not difficult to understand why cost control measures and cost reduction programs are given so much attention.

HOW BUDGETS AID IN COST CONTROL

In order to control costs properly, there must be a standard or a budget against which the actual costs can be compared. With a realistic budget, there is a basis for attaching significance to the costs that are not in agreement with the budgeted amounts. Budgets are an essential part of cost control, and in turn cost control leads to better budgets. Budgeting and cost control measures are very closely related. A well-prepared budget, for example, is the basis for cost control, and the information derived from an investigation of cost variances and the steps taken to eliminate these variances lead to the preparation of even better budgets. There is a circular effect as indicated below.

Both budgeting and cost control pertain to people and not to inanimate objects. Individuals within an organization who are responsible for certain functions and activities are expected to budget the costs that are authorized by them in carrying out their designated duties. The actual costs are then identified with the persons who authorize them, and each person in the organization assumes control over the costs that he has incurred, using his budget as a measuring standard. This approach to cost control, whereby each person budgets and controls his own costs, is designated as a *responsibility accounting system.*

Responsibility accounting when used properly is a powerful tool in controlling costs. Each person who has the authority to incur costs must study his operation thoroughly if he is to prepare an accurate and meaningful budget. Then he must exercise careful control over his costs if he is to meet the budget requirements. The budgets that are prepared individually must be reviewed and coordinated by a budgetary administrative group that in many cases operates under the jurisdiction of the controller.

THE FLEXIBLE BUDGET

Operations are not always conducted at the same level year after year. In one year, for example, a department may operate at 45,000 machine hours, and in another year at 50,000 machine hours. The variable costs, of course, are affected by the hours of operation. A budget that has been prepared for a given number of hours will not be sufficient.

As stated in Chapter 4, manufacturing overhead costs can be assigned to the products by using a rate per hour that has been computed from hours and costs budgeted for a normal level of operations. The concept of a normal or average level of plant utilization is applied to measure how effectively plant facilities are being used and is very important in itself.

It is also important to know what any particular cost should be at any level of operation. Therefore, a budget should be prepared for various levels, showing the expected costs for different levels of operation. A budget prepared on this basis is called a *flexible budget.* An example of a flexible budget is given below with costs broken down by variable and fixed components.

Flexible Budget

Machine hours budgeted	35,000	40,000	45,000	50,000
Variable costs:				
Materials and supplies	$105,000	$120,000	$135,000	$150,000
Wages	56,000	64,000	72,000	80,000
Repairs and maintenance	17,500	20,000	22,500	25,000
Heat and light	4,200	4,800	5,400	6,000
Total variable costs	$182,700	$208,800	$234,900	$261,000

Machine hours budgeted	35,000	40,000	45,000	50,000
Fixed costs:				
Salaries	$96,000	$96,000	$96,000	$96,000
Repairs and maintenance	28,000	28,000	28,000	28,000
Heat and light	15,000	15,000	15,000	15,000
Taxes and insurance	14,000	14,000	14,000	14,000
Depreciation	38,000	38,000	38,000	38,000
Total fixed costs	$191,000	$191,000	$191,000	$191,000
Total costs	$373,700	$399,800	$425,900	$452,000

If the company actually operated at 40,000 machine hours during the year, it operated at 10,000 hours below normal capacity if 50,000 machine hours are defined as normal capacity. A capacity variance can be determined to indicate how much of the fixed cost was not absorbed by the products manufactured as a result of assigning costs to the products by a rate determined for a normal capacity operation. In addition, all of the individual costs can be compared with the budget that is appropriate for the level attained; in this case, with the budget for 40,000 machine hours. To illustrate, actual costs for the year with operations at 40,000 hours are listed beside the costs budgeted for 40,000 hours, and the cost variances are given.

	Budget (40,000 machine hours)	Actual (40,000 machine hours)	Over (under) budget
Variable costs			
Materials and supplies	$120,000	$123,000	$ 3,000
Wages	64,000	63,500	(500)
Repairs and maintenance	20,000	19,600	(400)
Heat and light	4,800	5,600	800
Total variable costs	$208,800	$211,700	$ 2,900
Fixed costs			
Salaries	$ 96,000	$ 96,000	------
Repairs and maintenance	28,000	34,000	$ 6,000
Heat and light	15,000	14,700	(300)
Taxes and insurance	14,000	14,000	------
Depreciation	38,000	38,000	------
Total fixed costs	$191,000	$196,700	$ 5,700
Total costs	$399,800	$408,400	$ 8,600

THE TIME ELEMENT

Effective control over costs depends not only upon information with respect to cost variations but also upon how quickly the variations are detected and reported. For example, an operation may begin to deviate from a normal pattern early in the month with costs increasing beyond the budget limits. This condition may continue undetected for the entire month and may not be revealed until cost reports have been prepared and distributed in the following month. All this time the cost has been out of control with the variance increasing. Even after the variance is brought to the attention of those involved, it may still take time to investigate the condition and to bring it under control. As a result there may be a time lag of almost two months before the condition is corrected. It is like having a leaking faucet with the water loss increasing over a period of time. If at all possible, variations from a budgeted operation should be reported at or about the time they originate, and abnormalities in the operation should be corrected at once.

A computer can be quite helpful in that it can process data at a tremendous rate of speed, thus making it possible to report events soon after they take place. Corrections can then be made quickly, and variations that increase with time can be minimized. Ideally, of course, an operation should be under control at all times and should be automatically restored to balance when there is any tendency for the operation to stray off course. And this can be done if production is controlled by a computer. A slight variation can be detected right away if controls have been built into the computer program, and the operation can be corrected at the time the variation occurs.

LOCATING THE SIGNIFICANT VARIATIONS

Within limits variations in cost can be expected. As already pointed out in Chapter 3, a cost is not always at a set amount for a given number of hours. At best, an average cost is developed for budget and control purposes. Around this average there will be a certain amount of variation, and time and additional cost should not be expended to investigate normal variations from an average cost.

When management operates on a policy of concentrating attention on exceptions or variations from the expected pattern, it is operating on the principle of *management by exception*. This principle of control helps to conserve managerial time and directs it to the areas that should receive attention. Strangely enough, the problem of conserving managerial time may be more acute when data are processed by a computer. Difficulty arises if the computer is used to put out information with no thought being given to what type of information is useful. A computer can pour out a large volume of statistical information in a very short time, information that in many cases has very little value. In fact, an indiscriminate flood of information can be a handicap if managerial time is wasted in going over nonessential trivia. When a computer is used properly, only the significant facts are presented to management.

One of the big problems in cost control, of course, is to identify the variations that should be investigated and given attention. The absolute amount of the variation and the probability that it was caused by an abnormality of operation are factors in the selection process. A distinction between the significant and insignificant variations can be made by using the techniques described in Chapter 3 for the segregation of costs into variable and fixed classification. The costs are plotted on a graph with a line of regression drawn to fit the data. Line can then be drawn above and below the line of regression at a distance of plus and minus one standard deviation as shown in Figure 5-1.

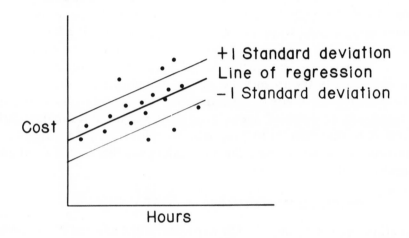

Figure 5-1

With a normal distribution of cost data, approximately 2/3 of the costs should lie within the zone formed by the lines for the standard deviation. There is a high probability (2 our of 3 times) that these variations are random variations that can be expected. Costs that lie outside of this zone may, of course, also vary randomly, but it is more likely that other factors are influencing this cost behavior. These are the costs that are identified for possible investigation.

If experience indicates that costs are often being investigated without good reason, the boundaries may be extended. Lines may be drawn for two standard deviations above and below the line of regression. In a normal cost distribution, approximately 95 percent of the data should lie within plus and minus two standard deviations. If a cost lies outside of this zone, it is very probable that some factor other than hours of operation has been responsible for the variation. At the same time, with a zone of two standard deviations above and below the line of regression, there is the risk of overlooking some cost variances that should be brought under control.

Only a few items of cost data were plotted on the graph given in Figure 5-1 to illustrate the general principle. In a practical situation, of course, very little significance can be attached to such a limited amount of data. Even with a reasonable quantity of data, the standard deviation serves only as a guide. About 95 percent of the time, data can be expected to lie within plus and minus two standard deviations from the line of regression. The probability of a cost beyond these limits resulting from random variation is relatively low, but it is still possible. There may be only a 5 percent probability, and a cost may be investigated only to find that it fits within this 5 percent area and was not influenced by other factors.

There is also the problem of correlation. Very little significance can be attached to variations in cost if there is a poor correlation between the cost and the hours of operation. Before attaching any importance to costs that lie outside of the zone determined by a standard deviation measurement, it should be established that there is a high degree of correlation between the cost and the hours of operation.

A computer may be used to plot cost data on a graph, to fit a line of regression to the data, and to fit lines for standard deviation measurements above and below the regression line. A chart may be prepared for each type of cost for each area of control. On each of these charts the r^2 may be shown to indicate the degree of correlation between the cost and the hours of operation. As time goes on, the cost pattern may shift; this trend can be detected and shown on the chart. Information derived from empirical cost data that have been processed to call attention to irregularities or to unusual situations can serve as a guideline in deciding whether or not a certain variation should be investigated.

WHEN TO INVESTIGATE A COST VARIATION

Some variation from the budget can be expected; if the amount of the variation falls within a given range, there is no reason to be concerned. Random variations that fall into the pattern should be disregarded. The more unusual variance that lies outside of the range may also be random, but it is more likely that some unexplained factor is responsible.

There is a risk attached to any action that is taken. If the cost variation is disregarded, unnecessary losses may accumulate in the future as a result of inadequate cost control measures. On the other hand, time and money may be spent to investigate a condition that is unlikely to be repeated.

Some guideline should be provided that can be used in deciding whether a cost variance should be investigated or not. Essentially, it is a problem of seeking a balance between the alternatives. The cost of investigating is compared with the cost of not investigating. The cost of not investigating is the present value of future cost variations, attributable to a condition that should be brought under control.

Cost to investigate = Present value of future cost variations.

If the cost to investigate is equal to the present value of the future cost variations, as shown above, a point of indifference is reached. The costs will be the same whether an investigation is made or not. This is a turning point or a form of break-even point.

If there is an inequality with the costs to investigate being greater than the present value of future cost variations, it will be better to accept the cost variation.

Cost to investigate   >   Present value of future cost variations

On the other hand, if the present value of future cost variations is greater than the cost to investigate, the cost should be investigated and brought under tighter control.

Cost to investigate   <   Present value of future cost variations

   The approach outlined above is oversimplified. As pointed out before, there is a risk of making the wrong decision. While this risk cannot be eliminated entirely, it can be quantified. What is the risk, for example, that a loss of a certain amount will be repeated? In other words, is this a random variation or is there some undetected factor influencing the cost? A probability should be placed on the assumption that a variation was caused by some abnormality in the operation, an abnormality that may possibly be identified and brought under control. Assume that costs have been arranged in a frequency distribution as shown in Figure 5-2 and that a certain cost identified as A on the curve has been brought to attention.

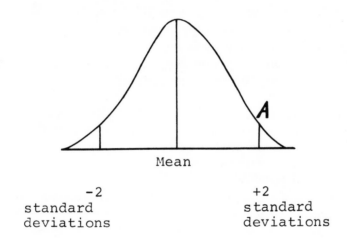

Mean

-2
standard
deviations

+2
standard
deviations

Figure 5-2

Cost A is two standard deviations above the mean. Approximately 95 percent of the cost data should lie within plus and minus two standard deviations from the mean. The remaining 5 percent will lie beyond these limits, with 2½ percent above and 2½ percent below. Cost A can be expected as a result of random variation about 2½ percent of the time. There is a 97½ percent probability, however, that this cost has been influenced by some factor that should perhaps be given attention.

   Not only should a probability be assigned to the variation but also the loss that can be expected from future repetitions should be estimated. A variation that has occurred once may occur year after year unless corrective measures are taken. The amount of any expected future variation may be difficult to estimate, but certain approaches to the problem may be useful. Perhaps the variation has occurred for several years and has been undetected or overlooked in the past. A review of past operations may reveal the magnitude of the loss and provide a guide for estimating future losses. As experience is developed, management should be able to identify potential trouble areas and estimate the probability of a recurrence of an abnormality and its probable cost.

The future variations as estimated must be reduced to a present value so that they can be compared with the present cost of investigation. A series of future dollar amounts can be placed on a present value basis by discounting these amounts at an appropriate rate of interest—the rate of return that a company can expect to earn from future operations.

THE DECISION TO INVESTIGATE

An example to show how a decision can be made is given below. Assume that the cost to investigate a variance has been estimated at $200. The variance itself amounts to $100, and there is only a 3 percent probability that such a variance is random. This means that there is a 97 percent probability that the variance is not random. The company, in this illustration, expects a 30 percent return before income taxes, and the cost variation is reduced to a present value on this basis. Arbitrarily, a ten-year period has been selected for determination of the present value. This period may be extended or reduced according to circumstances, or a perpetual rate may be selected if desired. For all practical purposes, an assumption that the variance may be repeated for each of ten years should be sufficient. The factors are reduced to symbols to form an equation.

Cost of investigation	= I	= $200.
Cost variation	= CV	= $100.
Probability of a non-random variance	= Pr	= .97
*Present value of $1 spent each year for		
10 years with interest at 30%	= Pv	= 3.092

*Obtained from a table of present value of $1 received for N years.

$$I = Pr \times Pv \times Cv$$

A point of indifference is reached if the equation balances. If there is unbalance, a decision should be made to accept the less costly alternative.

$$\$200 \ < \ .97 \times 3.092 \times \$100$$
$$\$200 \ < \ \$299.92$$

The cost should be investigated inasmuch as the expected loss on a present value basis is greater than the cost of investigation.

Obviously the cost of investigation itself must be held to a minimum, otherwise many costs that should be given attention will be disregarded because of the high cost associated with investigation.

In a practical application, it may not always be easy to estimate the discount rate to be used to place a present value on future dollar costs. The discount rate is not necessarily the rate that is currently being earned. Instead, it is the rate of return expected from operations in the future, and this rate can be derived from economic forecasts using the best information available. There is also uncertainty with respect to the number of fiscal periods in which a cost variation will be repeated or as to the amount of the variation in any particular year. Precise estimates cannot be expected, but this approach to the problem will tend to reduce both the cost variations and the costs of investigation.

SUMMARY

One of the big problems in cost control is the identification of the cost variations that should be investigated. This problem may be approached by fitting a line of regression to empirical cost data and by forming a zone equal to plus and minus one or two standard deviations from this line. If there is a high degree of correlation between the cost and the hours of operation, a cost lying outside of this zone should be considered for investigation.

Before making a final decision, the cost to investigate a cost variation should be compared with the probable future variations stated on a present value basis. If the cost of investigation is higher than the expected loss, it would be better to accept the possibility of future cost variations.

6

Controlling the Cost of Materials

The control over materials cost deserves special attention not only because the cost of materials is often substantial, but also because of the types of problems that are encountered from the time that materials are ordered from suppliers until they are delivered to customers as part of a final product. In addition to the cost of the material itself, there are the costs of administration in this area and the costs of handling the material; and these costs, too, may be relatively significant. Decisions must be made, decisions that involve a balancing of alternatives in an attempt to find the one that offers the most advantages at the least possible cost.

Often the problem of controlling spoilage and shrinkage loss in production is critical. Losses in production in many cases may be excessive because of poor purchasing practices. If materials are perishable the suppliers' delivery schedules must be carefully synchronized with production schedules. Apparent savings that may be realized by purchasing lower quality materials or by dealing with less reliable suppliers can be more than offset by losses in production. In short, the materials procurement function must be designed to meet the peculiar needs of production. Materials losses attributable to production itself can be controlled by following the general principles of cost control discussed in Chapter 5.

It is not possible to discuss all of the problems of materials cost control in this chapter, but a few of the more critical problems of materials procurement are identified below.

1. The selection of a supplier.
2. Materials handling costs.
3. Inventory protection.
4. The economic order size.
5. Purchasing in large lot sizes.

85

THE SELECTION OF A SUPPLIER

A company that has been in business for many years has usually established a long-term working relationship with suppliers of materials and services. Over the years a company will generally work out a policy with its suppliers with respect to the quality of materials, sizes, delivery dates, and adjustments for defects or errors in shipment. A reliable supplier who can furnish the desired quantity of material that meets the quality standards and who can furnish it as needed contributes a great deal to the success of its customers. In a sense, the supplier and the customer are in business together almost as if they were partners.

Many long-term relationships between suppliers and customers are mutually advantageous, but this cannot be taken for granted. Habit and inertia may help to perpetuate a relationship that is no longer beneficial because of changes in the policies and personnel of either company.

In selecting a supplier, or in re-evaluating a present supplier, price is only one of the many factors to be considered. Obviously, price must be related to quality. An apparent saving in the acquisition of materials by purchasing solely on a price basis may be overbalanced if the materials are expensive to use in production. A cheaper material may break more easily, or it may be difficult to work with in the manufacturing process.

There is also a problem of dependability. A supplier may deliver material that meets specification standards, and the price may be reasonable, but perhaps he cannot deliver the material as scheduled. As a result, there may be unbalances in the purchasing company's production schedule or dislocations in the receiving area.

EXTRA SERVICES FROM A SUPPLIER

A supplier who charges higher prices may be favored because of extra services furnished and the help that he can give under emergency conditions. There may be various kinds of services, including, for example, special deliveries of materials when needed and the cooperation of a representative of the supplier in deciding how the materials may be used to the best advantage. These extra services are highly important and in some cases are essential. Often it will be difficult to measure their value in monetary terms.

Indirectly, the services may be valued at the differential cost that a company is willing to pay in order to obtain them. For example, two suppliers may be able to furnish identical materials. One of the suppliers helps the customer with production problems, and the other supplier doesn't. The supplier who offers this extra service charges $.15 more per unit of material. The customer ordinarily uses 100,000 units of this material each year and purchases it from the more expensive supplier. Apparently, the purchaser is willing to pay the premium price because he places a value of at least $15,000 on the help that he receives with production problems.

Value of additional service	$\geq$	additional cost of materials
Value of additional service	$\geq$	100,000 units x $.15 difference in cost per unit
Value of additional service	$\geq$	$15,000 a year.

These services may be valued at more than $15,000 a year if the buyer is willing to pay a cost differential of more than $.15 a unit or if he purchases more than 100,000 units.

BREAK EVEN AND THE SELECTION OF SUPPLIERS

In comparing suppliers, the relevant factors should be identified and assigned monetary values wherever possible. Then equations or inequalities can be established for the purpose of making cost comparisons. By using an equation form, management is forced to approach the problem in a logical way and is less likely to leave out factors that may be highly relevant in making a decision.

An example is given to illustrate the break-even approach to the problem.

	Suppliers	
	A	*B*
Unit cost of materials	$ 1.60	$ 1.80
Number of units required each year	100,000	100,000
Value of services given to production (measured as annual saving in production cost)	8,000	12,000
Extra cost identified with late deliveries (additional cost of handling materials received after regular hours)	2,000	1,000

The data are assembled in the form of an equation or inequality. Everything else being equal, the less expensive alternative will be selected.

The value of the services given by one supplier is part of the cost of selecting the other supplier. In decision making, this conception of cost is very important. If an advantage that can be derived from a particular course of action is sacrificed by selecting another course of action, this advantage becomes the cost of the alternative selected. This type of cost is called an *opportunity cost.* It is not an incurred cost that can be measured in the accounting records, but it is a very real cost from a decision-making point of view. After a decision has been made, however, the opportunity cost is no longer relevant. The opportunity cost concept also applies in personal situations. For example, you may have the opportunity to earn $50 by working on a particular evening. Instead, you decide to take your wife out to dinner at a cost of $20. The cost of this decision is $70: the cost of the dinner of $20 plus the sacrifice of $50 that could have been earned by working extra time.

Returning to the example, an inequality is established so that the factors can be brought together to reach a decision.

| | Cost of buying from Supplier A | $\neq$ | Cost of buying from Supplier B | |

Cost of buying from Supplier A			$\neq$	*Cost of buying from Supplier B*		
Materials cost	Value of services from Supplier B	Cost of late delivery		Materials cost	Value of services from Supplier A	Cost of late delivery
$160,000	+ $12,000	+ $2,000		$180,000	+ $8,000	+ $1,000
	Cost of buying from Supplier A				Cost of buying from Supplier B	
	$174,000				$189,000	

Note that the value of the services that can be received from one supplier is an opportunity cost of buying from the other supplier. In this example, if there are no other relevant factors, Supplier A should be selected.

Sometimes the problem of selecting a supplier extends to other areas. For example, a supplier may also be a customer and will not continue as a customer without supplying the materials. The profits to be derived in dealing with the supplier as a customer must then be compared with the cost disadvantage, if any, in selecting the customer as a supplier. Assume, in the previous example, that Supplier B is also a customer and contributed annual profits of $40,000 to the total operation. Under these conditions, Supplier B should be selected.

Cost disadvantage of buying from Supplier B		Profit advantage of selling to Supplier B
$15,000	$<$	$40,000
($189,000 – $174,000)		

MATERIALS HANDLING COSTS

In many cases the costs of handling materials will be inconsequential. But in other circumstances, material may be bulky and when received may require the work of several men with the aid of various types of equipment such as fork lift trucks, cranes, bulldozers, conveyor belts, etc. Alternate methods of handling materials should be compared for efficiency of operation and cost. This problem, like the problem of selecting suppliers, can be set up in equation form. The costs of labor and equipment for one method can then be compared with the corresponding costs for another method.

However, if equipment is a factor in making the decision, the decision becomes a capital investment decision (which is discussed in Chapter 12). Equipment is expected to yield benefits over a period of years, and in order to make a valid comparison, the benefits expected in future years must be placed on a present value basis before being compared with the present cost of the equipment.

INVENTORY PROTECTION

After materials are received, there is the problem of protection; not merely the protection of insurance coverage, but also protection through the control of materials use. Without adequate controls, materials may be wasted or misappropriated with the result that materials cost is higher than it should be. In addition, materials may not be available when needed for production, and production schedules may be delayed and customers disappointed. Ordinarily, materials are stored in enclosed areas and released only upon presentation of authorized requisitions. A formal control over the issuance of materials provides more accurate accountability and tends to reduce careless waste and improper use. For many types of materials, a control over issuance is necessary. However, there is a cost attached to this control measure, and strict control may not always be desirable.

One company made a study of this problem and found that some low value items that are frequently used should be exempt from this control. These items, designated as expense items, were placed in bins located outside the inventory enclosure and thus made available to all employees. The cost to maintain perpetual inventory records and to release the materials upon requisition, not to speak of the inconvenience, was greater than the expected loss from a lack of control.

Without question, inventories should be stored properly to minimize spoilage and damage and should be covered by adequate insurance, and, in addition, should be controlled as to use in most cases. At the same time it must be remembered that control in itself has a cost. In some situations it may be more economical to accept the risk of loss than to pay the cost to have controls. Once again it is a breakeven application, comparing the costs of control against the possible losses.

ECONOMIC ORDER SIZE

A certain amount of materials inventory must be maintained at all times to meet production schedules. And this inventory must be in balance. There is no point in having an overstock of one type of material if there is a shortage in another. A chain is only as strong as its weakest link. If two types of material are used to manufacture a certain product line, a limitation on production is imposed by the material that is relatively scarce.

Ordinarily, minimum inventory levels are established for each type of material. The minimum inventory level is equal to the consumption expected from the time an order is placed with a supplier until the material is received, with some allowance made for unusual delays or above average consumption.

If inventories are maintained at basic minimum levels, the company has a smaller investment in inventory and can apply its resources for other purposes. The return that can be earned from resources that would otherwise be invested in inventory is the opportunity cost of holding large inventory investments.

Part of the cost of holding a large inventory is the sacrifice of the return that can be earned from resources that would otherwise be available for profitable investment if they were not frozen in the form of inventory. In addition to this opportunity cost, there is the cost of insurance and the cost of storage itself. The cost of storage may include another opportunity cost—the advantage that could be obtained if the storage space devoted to inventories were available for other purposes. Also, if inventories are stored for a long period of time, there is the risk of deterioration and spoilage.

Seemingly, inventories should be cut to a minimum; but this too has its disadvantages. With low inventories, orders will have to be placed more frequently and materials will have to be received and stored more often. This can also be expensive. Then there is the risk of running out of materials at some critical point. If large quantities of materials are not available, the products may have to be manufactured in smaller batches. This means that machines used in production may have to be set up more frequently because of changes in the production runs. This same problem is also encountered with low inventories of finished products. There is a cost attached to changing the machines for different production runs, and, in addition, a slowdown in the production process. This, too, has a cost.

AN EQUATION TO BALANCE ORDER AND STORAGE COSTS

It is apparent that either approach to the inventory problem has its advantages and disadvantages. Storage costs are higher when larger inventories are maintained, and ordering costs are higher when smaller inventories are maintained. Ideally, a balance should be maintained so that the combined cost will be minimized.

Many textbooks that deal with inventory control give the following formula for the computation of the quantity that should be purchased on each order to minimize the combined costs of storing and ordering materials.

$$Q = \frac{\sqrt{2DO}}{S}$$

Q = Optimum quantity per order
D = Annual demand
O = Cost per order placed
S = Storage cost per unit per year

In working with an inventory of finished product, the cost to set up a new production run may be substituted for the cost to place an order.

Essentially, this formula has been developed from a break-even type of equation. The basic principle remains the same. For example, in the very first chapter it was stated that a company breaks even when:

Revenue = Expenses

A company also breaks even in a decisional situation when:

The cost of selecting one alternative = The cost of selecting the other alternative

As more orders are placed during the year, the costs to order increase but the costs to store decrease. Conversely, when fewer orders are placed, the costs to order decrease but the cost to store increase. When the costs are in balance, the combined cost is usually minimized. In certain cases, however, this will not be the minimum point. For example, if the cost to place each order increases or decreases as more orders are placed, if the cost to store increases at an increasing rate, or if the price of the material varies with quantities purchased, the minimum cost will not necessarily be at the point of balance between order and storage costs.

The conventional formula can be developed from equations as shown below.

$$\text{The cost to order} = \frac{\text{Annual demand}}{\text{Optimum quantity per order}} \times \text{Cost per order}$$

or

$$\text{The cost to order} = \frac{DO}{Q.}$$

The annual demand divided by the optimum quantity per order yields the number of orders per year. And the number of orders per year when multiplied by the cost per order yields the total cost of placing orders during the year.

$$\text{The cost to store} = \frac{\text{Optimum quantity per order}}{2} \times \text{Storage cost per unit}$$

or

$$\text{The cost to store} = \frac{QS}{2}$$

The optimum quantity per order is divided by 2 to give a rough average of the number of units in stock, assuming a uniform flow of units into production. The average number of units in the inventory is multiplied by the unit storage cost to yield the total storage cost for the year.

$$\text{The cost to order} = \text{The cost to store}$$

$$\frac{DO}{Q} = \frac{QS}{2}$$

Solve for Q, the optimum order quantity.

$$DO = \frac{Q^2 S}{2}$$

$$Q^2 S = 2DO$$

$$Q^2 = \frac{2DO}{S}$$

$$Q = \frac{\sqrt{2DO}}{S}$$

AN ILLUSTRATION OF OPTIMUM ORDER SIZE

An example is given to show how the optimum lot size can be determined. The cost of $8 to store each unit for the year includes insurance, the cost of storage space, and the sacrifice of a rate of return that could be earned by resources committed to inventory investment.

Q = optimum quantity per order (unknown)
D = annual demand, 1,000 units of material
O = cost to place each order, $40
S = storage cost per unit per year, $8

$$Q = \frac{\sqrt{2DO}}{S}$$

$$Q = \frac{\sqrt{2 \times 1,000 \times 40}}{8}$$

$$Q = \sqrt{10,000}$$

$$Q = 100$$

If the annual demand is 1,000 units and if 100 units are to be acquired on each order, 10 orders must be placed during the year.

A proof of the computation follows.

Number of orders	Number of units per order (approx.)	Average inventory (approx.)	Storage cost	Order cost	Combined cost
7	143	72	$576	$280	$856
8	125	62	496	320	816
9	111	56	448	360	808
10	100	50	400	400	800
11	91	46	368	440	808
12	83	42	336	480	816
13	77	39	312	520	832

If 7 orders are placed during the year, it will be necessary to order approximately 143 units each time if 1,000 units are required for the year. On the average, assuming a uniform rate of withdrawal, half of the number ordered will be in the inventory, or approximately 72 units. If it costs $8 to store a unit, the total storage cost will be $576. The total cost to order will be equal to 7 orders multiplied by the $40 cost per order, or $280. The combined cost for 7 orders is $856. Similar computations will be made for the other numbers of orders. As the number of orders increases, the costs to order increase. However, with more frequent orders, there are fewer units in the inventory and a lower cost for storage. With 10 orders, the cost to order is equal to the cost to store, and the combined costs are minimized at $800.

PURCHASING IN LARGE LOT SIZES

The economic order size can often be computed as shown, but sometimes there will be complicating factors. In the example given, it was assumed that any number of units of material could be purchased at a certain price. This will not always be true. A supplier may grant price concessions to customers who purchase in round lot sizes. With quantity discounts available, it may be more economical to buy in round lots as defined by the supplier and to accept the higher storage costs.

Assume, for example, that the economic order quantity for a given material has been computed at 500 units.

Q = optimum order size, 500 units
D = annual demand, 10,000 units
O = cost per order placed, $60
S = storage cost per year, 24% of average inventory investment
P = cost of each unit of material, $20

Cost to order   =   Cost to store

$$\frac{DO}{Q} \qquad\qquad \frac{QS}{2}$$

$$\frac{10,000 \times \$60}{500} \quad = \quad \frac{500 \times \$20 \times .24}{2}$$

$$\$1,200 \quad = \quad \$1,200$$

The combined cost to order and store this material is $2,400. Assuming no price differential for quantity purchases, 500 units should be purchased on each of 20 orders placed during the year.

However, if the supplier charges $15 for each unit when the lot sizes are in multiples of 600 units and charges $20 a unit for any lot size of less than 600 units, the results may be different. Price may be introduced as a factor by extending the equation concept to include the cost of the materials themselves under both alternatives.

P = price per unit, small lots, $20
C = price per unit, 600-unit lots, $15
Q = size of small lot, 500 units
R = size of large lot, 600 units

$DC + \dfrac{DO}{R} + \dfrac{RS}{2} =$ Cost of round lots for the year including costs to order and store.

$DP + \dfrac{DO}{Q} + \dfrac{QS}{2} =$ Cost of 500-unit orders for the year
including costs to order and store.

If the total costs are equal, there is a point of indifference—a break-even point. Each alternative would have the same cost, and it wouldn't matter which one was selected. An inequality, however, indicates that the less costly alternative should be selected.

$$DC + \frac{DO}{R} + \frac{RS}{2} = \text{ or } \neq DP + \frac{DO}{Q} + \frac{QS}{2}$$

$$(10,000 \times \$15) + \left(\frac{10,000 \times 60}{600}\right) + \left(\frac{600 \times 15 \times .24}{2}\right) = \text{ or } \neq$$

$$(10,000 \times \$20) \ + \ \frac{(10,000 \times 60)}{(\qquad 500 \qquad)} + \frac{(500 \times 20 \times .24)}{(\qquad 2 \qquad)}$$

$$\$152,080 \neq \$202,400.$$

In this situation, with a price differential as stated, the company should not follow the conventional economic lot-size formula and purchase in lots of 500 units. Instead, purchases should be made in lots of 600 units each. Sometimes the price structure may be more complicated, with various prices for different quantity brackets. However, the principle remains the same. The cost of the optimum order size under one price condition can be compared with the cost of large purchases, with various alternatives compared in a search for the best order size. A computer can be helpful in more complex situations, with different values assigned to the variables in various combinations, testing one alternative against another until the best solution is found.

SUMMARY

Materials control problems generally receive a great deal of attention because of the substantial cost of materials and the significant part that materials play in the successful operation of a company. Careful attention must be given to every aspect of the operation to be sure that a subtle but very important factor has not been overlooked. The materials control operation includes everything from the selection of competent suppliers to the incorporation of the materials into the final product.

It will not be easy to place precise values on all of the factors, but a quantitative approach to the problem provides an orderly and disciplined analysis of the operation. Decisions, of course, cannot be based solely on formulas and equations or inequalities. Nevertheless, the break-even type of equation can help to solve some of the problems, and at the very least is a step toward solution, providing management with the economic data that can be used along with other information in making a final decision.

7

Increasing Profit Potential from Improved Sales Promotion and Distribution

Both production and sales are highly important to the successful operation of a business, and one function cannot be said to be more or less important than the other. An efficient manufacturing division that can furnish the products desired by the customers as they are needed simplifies the task of selling. The sales division lives within the limits imposed by the manufacturing operation, and a failure to sell may be chargeable to production if satisfactory products cannot be produced and delivered according to schedule. In turn, the best efforts of a manufacturing division are wasted if the product lines are not promoted and distributed as they should be.

Frequently a discussion of how costs can be used to control and plan operations is centered around the manufacturing operation, with relatively little attention being given to the sales division. There is a general approach to planning and control problems that applies to all areas of business, and manufacturing applications can often be adapted to serve the needs of sales management and the needs of other functional areas. There are some peculiarities in selling, however, that deserve special attention.

SALES AND THE MEASUREMENT PROBLEM

Planning and control in the area of sales is somewhat difficult because of the human factor, and for that reason there is a general reluctance to make evaluations on a quantitative basis. The sales division forms the contacts with the customers for the most part and as a result is more exposed to the problems of dealing with people. In dealing with people it is not easy to make precise measurements in terms of dollars or in terms of some other measurable unit. It is quite difficult, for example, to make an exact computation of the increase in sales revenue that can be expected from a given increase in advertising expenditures. In manufacturing there may be some difficulty in computing the output of product from given production inputs, but this is much easier

95

than measuring results that depend upon the preferences of customers and changes in the social environment.

While it is admittedly difficult to place values on factors that seem to be beyond measurement, the problem itself cannot be avoided. Some decision has to be made, even if it is made on an intuitive basis, and better decisions can be made by considering the quantitative measurements, using approximations whenever necessary. At the very least, the risk is defined.

A few of the problems in the sales area are examined in this chapter, with particular emphasis placed upon the measurement aspects. These problems are listed below.

1. Measuring the effect of advertising and sales promotion.
2. Packaging the product.
3. Evaluating the calls by sales representatives.
4. Selecting distribution channels.
5. Estimating the demand for perishable products.
6. Selecting the most economical routes of distribution.

MEASURING THE EFFECT OF ADVERTISING AND SALES PROMOTION

Success in marketing rarely depends upon one factor alone but rather upon several factors such as advertising, promotion, personal calls by sales representatives, services to customers, product reputation, and convenience. With various factors used in combination, it is somewhat difficult to isolate any one factor and to measure its effect on sales.

In the case of advertising, fixed dollar amounts are often budgeted not for the purpose of increasing sales volume but to maintain it. The general public must constantly be reminded of the product line, and will tend to associate products with certain types of advertising. A particular television program, for example, may be sponsored regularly by a company as a matter of course. To some extent advertising becomes institutionalized and in time creates an image for the company and its products. Inasmuch as advertising provides sales momentum, there is obviously a reluctance to interfere with fixed budgets for fear of an adverse effect on sales.

As a general rule, advertising expenditures should not be budgeted at a stated percentage of sales revenue. Sales volume is dependent to some extent upon advertising; if advertising is reduced when sales decline, sales volume may be reduced even further. In fact, it may be argued that advertising should be increased when sales volume declines.

Measuring the Effect of Advertising

Ideally, a correlation between advertising expenditures and sales volume should be established. To obtain a realistic measurement of correlation, however, all other influences on sales should be held constant. If this isn't feasible, perhaps the effect of the *total* sales effort on sales volume can be measured. The total approach is particularly appropriate when advertising is followed by personal calls and special promotions.

It may be possible to measure the effect of increments in advertising by making market tests in limited areas, or the effect of advertising may be isolated to an extent by special sales promotions. A product, for example, may be offered at a reduced price upon presentation of a coupon or at some advertised location. Precise measurements cannot be expected, but controlled tests may reveal a general relationship between increased advertising expenditures and increased sales volume.

There are several different ways to advertise, and part of the problem is to select the most effective advertising program or programs from among those that are available. Past experience and customary practice in the industry may provide information that will be helpful in making a decision. If information cannot be developed from past experience, tests may be made on a limited basis, as stated in the preceding paragraph, to determine the possible effect of a more extensive advertising program. In making these decisions, management must also consider the reaction of competitors and the possible impact on the market that will result from their countering moves.

Essentially the selection of an advertising program is another version of the conventional break-even problem. Sales volume in itself is not important, however. It is the profit contribution that is important, and expected increases in sales volume should be translated into expected increases in profit contribution. The break-even point is the point at which increases in advertising cost equal increases in the resulting profit contribution. The advertising program that offers the best profit potential after all factors have been considered is the program that should be selected.

Tests may reveal that the profit contribution will rise more rapidly at first and tend to level off as advertising is used more intensively. Furthermore, the profits derived from advertising may appear several months after the advertising expenditures have been made. The profit lag effect must be estimated in evaluating the total effectiveness of an advertising budget. A graph is given in Figure 7-1 to show a possible relationship between profit contributions and advertising expenditures, with all profit contributions from the related advertising included.

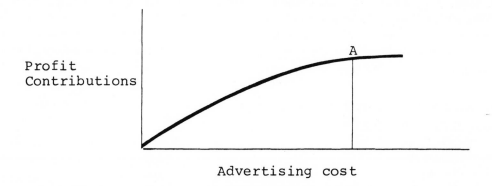

Figure 7-1

At point A it is assumed that the expected profit contribution from increased advertising is equal to the increased advertising cost. This is the break-even point.

Profit contribution from increased advertising = Additional advertising cost

In practice, of course, there is uncertainty, and advertising will probably not be extended to the break-even point in an attempt to optimize profits. The risk of making inaccurate estimates will tend to be a restraining factor.

PACKAGING THE PRODUCT

The container used for packaging a product should not be looked upon as being merely a container. It is also a part of the total advertising program. Obviously, the container must be functional and must protect the product from leakage and spoilage. In addition, it should be designed for customer appeal and for product identification. Sometimes other product lines may be advertised on the labels. Color, shape, size, and the type of container material such as glass, aluminum, steel, or plastic will often play an important part in the selection of a container.

Before selecting a container, tests may be made in certain market areas to determine the customer reaction. Various alternatives may be tested with costs of the container offset against customer response in each case. A comparison of alternatives provides an economic basis for selection, from which it is possible to go further and to consider changes in style, competition in the market, improvements in container technology, and other factors not included in the economic analysis.

EVALUATING THE CALLS OF SALES REPRESENTATIVES

In many lines of business, the sales representative is the most important man in the organization. He is the company in the eyes of the customer. If the sales representative is the key to obtaining orders from customers, then his time must be used to the best advantage. Analysis may reveal that too much time is being spent on marginal customers who either buy very little or buy less profitable lines. Perhaps profits can be improved by shifting time to the development of new customers or to the customers who bring more profits to the company. Time may be reallocated on the basis of reports showing profit results and the time and cost to make the sale.

Assume, for example, that a sales representative has the following alternatives with equal probabilities (developed from past experience) that the sales results will be as indicated:

Customer A

Expected profit contribution from orders placed		$4,000
Less cost to make the sale:		
Travel cost	$ 500	
Entertainment	600	
Commissions	400	
*Cost of time expended	1,600	3,100
Profit contribution, less cost to make sale		$ 900

<u>Customer B</u>

Expected profit contribution from orders placed		$6,000
Less cost to make the sale:		
Travel cost	$ 200	
Commissions	600	
*Cost of time expended	2,700	3,500
Profit contribution, less cost to make the sale		$2,500

In the example given, Customer B is a more profitable customer. The profit contribution expected by Customer A of $900 becomes an additional opportunity cost of selecting Customer B. The net advantage in selecting Customer B is $1,600 ($2,500 - $900).

Profit contribution, Customer B		Profit contribution, Customer A
$2,500	>	$900

Unfortunately, it will not always be easy to make these comparisons in practice. Long-range considerations may upset the results of an analysis made on a short-run basis. For example, time must be taken to develop new customers, and although the immediate results are unfavorable, there is future potential. Perhaps the customer is growing and will soon be in a position to place large and profitable orders. Or a customer may be trying the product on a trial basis and, if satisfied, will purchase larger quantities in the future. In setting up equations or inequalities for comparison, the long-term factors should be quantified if possible or at the very least should be evaluated on a judgment basis.

Under certain conditions it may be possible to measure future profit potential on a present value basis. Information derived from past experience may serve as a guide in placing values on the variables. If reasonable values can be assigned to the future expected profits and if these profits can be stated on a present value basis, the area requiring intuitive judgment can be reduced even further.

It is easier to make a decision, of course, when a customer can be identified as one who always buys small quantities of low profit items and when there is no prospect of change. In these circumstances the break-even type of analysis sorts out the less profitable customers and provides a reliable basis for a redistribution of sales time.

METHODS OF DISTRIBUTION

There is also the problem of how products should be distributed to the customers. Conventional practice and the nature of the product or service will obviously play an important part, but options will most likely be available. For example, should the company advertise and solicit orders by mail? Is it better to distribute through franchised outlets, through company-controlled outlets, or through independent

---

*Combination of fixed salary for the sales representative and the opportunity cost of the sacrifice of profits that may be realized by working with other potential customers in the area. If the opportunity cost is relatively large, the company should consider the need for additional sales representatives.

dealers? Even after a distribution channel or a combination of channels has been selected, there is the additional problem of deciding how distribution can be handled to the best advantage.

Once again a comparison can be made. The costs to distribute by each method can be compared with the expected profit contribution, and the best alternative or combination of alternatives can be selected. The measurement problem in this area is also clouded by uncertainty. For example, will deliveries be made according to schedule? The sale itself may depend upon the time of delivery. Weather and other unknown factors may complicate the problem. A study of past experience may be used as a guide in placing probabilities on the reliability of a delivery system, and management can weigh the additional cost of relative certainty against the risks associated with a less reliable and less expensive system.

The selection of a delivery system may also be included as a part of the problem of selecting the best routes for distribution of the product. Later in this chapter a model is developed showing how the transportation problem is handled by many large companies. If costs can be identified with the alternatives, it is possible to solve for the most economic solution.

ESTIMATING THE DEMAND FOR PERISHABLE PRODUCTS

The problem of distribution is somewhat more complicated when the products are perishable. The product or service must be available when the customer wants it, or a sale is lost. And the product or service by definition cannot be stored. If a surplus of the product or service remains, it will deteriorate with time and must be disposed of either at a loss or under less favorable conditions than if it were sold according to original plan.

Examples of Perishable Products and Services

One often thinks of food when thinking of perishable goods and services, but other industries are also faced with this problem. For example, a news dealer must stock current newspapers and magazines. And a transportation company, for example an airline, does not sell a tangible product but offers a perishable service. If too many aircraft are provided along a given route, there is the cost of flying unused seating capacity. The fixed cost of providing a flight is high, and if there are not enough passengers, the flight may be unprofitable. On the other hand, if sufficient service is not available, customers will be turned away and will either go to competing carriers or seek other means of transport. The airlines must be ready for service when the customer is ready to travel.

Studies have been made by various companies to determine how much of a perishable product or service should be available to serve the customers while at the same time minimizing the losses from an excess supply. Experience may provide information that can be used to predict demand on a probability basis. For example, assume that a study of demand for the past 500 days reveals that 30 units of product are ordered on 150 of those days. On this basis, it may be stated that there is a 30 percent probability of a demand for 30 units. Similarly, other probabilities based on relevant past experience can be developed for various levels of demand. In this example, it is assumed that on another 150 days there was a demand for 31 units, and on 200 days there was a demand for 32 units. The probabilities have been computed as shown.

Demand (number of units)	Computation of probability	Probability
30	150/500	.30
31	150/500	.30
32	200/500	.40

Presumably, the best action would be to order 32 units and make the correct decision 40 percent of the time. But other factors must be considered, such as the profit contribution per unit of product and the loss that will be incurred on surplus units.

Assume in this case that each unit of product sold contributes $5 to profits, that each unsold unit of product is thrown away, and that it costs $4 to make each unit. A tabulation is given below to show the net profit contributions expected from providing various quantities of product.

Alternative Quantities Available
(Units of product)

Estimated Demand	Demand probabilities	30 Profit contribution	30 Probable contribution	31 Profit contribution	31 Probable contribution	32 Profit contribution	32 Probable contribution
30	.3	$150	$45	$146	$43.80	$142	$42.60
31	.3	150	45	155	46.50	151	45.30
32	.4	150	60	155	62.00	160	64.00
Expected values of the decisions			$150		$152.30		$151.90

If only 30 units are provided for the market, the profit contribution will be $150 (30 x $5). No units will be thrown away, but there may be disappointed customers.

If 31 units are provided, one unit must be thrown away if only 30 units are ordered by the customers. The profit in this case will be $146 ($150 - $4). When there is a demand for 31 or 32 units, the profit will be $155 (31 x $5). The expected profit from this decision, with probabilities taken into account, is $152.30. (Multiply the profit effect by the probability of each demand and add the results.)

If 32 units are provided, units will have to be thrown away if only 30 or 31 units are ordered by the customers. Two units must be thrown away if there is a demand for only 30 units, and the profit will be $142 ($150 - $8). If there is a demand for 31 units, one unit must be thrown away and the profit will be $151 ($155 - $4). The profit weighted by the probabilities amounts to $151.90.

The best decision in this example is to stock 31 units. According to the information that is available, the profits will be higher over the long run when 31 units are provided.

If the company had perfect knowledge of demand, the units would be stocked accordingly. There would be no disappointed customers and no losses from the disposal of excess units. The expected profit with perfect information is computed below.

Actual demand and units provided	Demand probabilities	Profit effect	Probable profit effect
30	.3	$150	$ 45.00
31	.3	155	46.50
32	.4	160	64.00
Expected profit with certainty			$155.50

With perfect information on customer demand, profits can be improved. Perhaps the company can have this advance knowledge by taking firm advance orders from the customers. The value of perfect information is equal to the difference between the expected profit with certainty and the best expected profit with uncertainty.

Expected profit with certainty		Expected profit with uncertainty		Value of perfect information
$155.50	—	$152.30	=	$3.20

The company can afford to pay up to $3.20 for perfect information. That is, the cost to obtain firm orders in advance must be less than $3.20. This is a fulcrum or break-even point in deciding how much should be spent to obtain firm reservations.

In the example given, small amounts were used to illustrate the general principle, but the principle remains the same, of course, with larger and more realistic amounts or with more demand alternatives.

If desired, an opportunity cost may be identified with sales lost by failing to serve all potential customers. There is then a cost of undersupply as well as a cost of oversupply.

Some companies may find that the importance of giving service to all customers may outweigh the losses that can be expected from an oversupply. Each situation must be examined according to the circumstances. For example, is a product or service essential or does the customer have a satisfactory alternative? And what is the effect on future profits if customers must be turned away?

SELECTING ROUTES OF DISTRIBUTION

Options are also available in delivering the products to customers. Some companies have regional warehouses, thus making it easier and more economical to distribute the products to customers located in various parts of the country. Customers who are approximately an equal distance from two or more warehouses may be served about as conveniently from one of the warehouses as from another. Or if there is a shortage of supply at one warehouse, alternate shipping routes may be selected to serve the customers from a more distant warehouse. And there are various methods of transport such as air freight, commercial trucks, rental trucks, ships, or a combination of carriers. Costs are identified with each shipping alternative available, and routes are selected that will minimize the total cost.

The Transportation Model

A logical process has been developed in operations research for determining the most economical shipping routes. This process is a linear programming application and is referred to as the *transportation model* or as the *transportation problem.*

A very simple illustration is given to show how a problem of this type can be solved. A two-dimensional array is set up with sources of distribution on a vertical scale and customer locations on a horizontal scale. The cost to ship a unit of product from any source to any location is entered in the upper left-hand corner of the appropriate box in the array as shown in Figure 7-2.

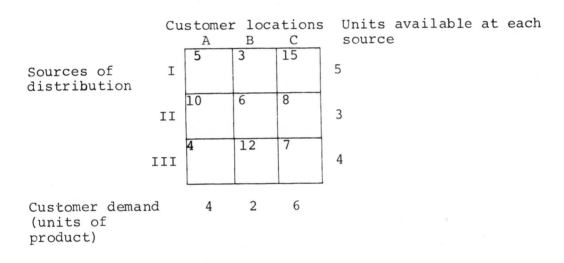

Figure 7-2

The cost, for example, of shipping a unit from Source I to Location A is $5 per unit, as shown in the upper left-hand box. The row totals are the total units available from any given source, and the column totals are the total units required at any given location.

The first step in searching for an optimum solution is to prepare a feasible solution, which is then tested to determine whether or not improvements can be made. The northwest corner (the upper left-hand box) is the point of entry in developing a feasible solution. Customer A is supplied with as much product as he requires, subject to the limitation of the amount available from Source I. The next box in the row (I-B) is then completed in the same way, with the row requirements being fulfilled subject to the total column requirements. Move across the row to exhaust the row requirements before going on to the next row. The number of units to be shipped by a certain route is entered in the center of the box as shown in Figure 7-3.

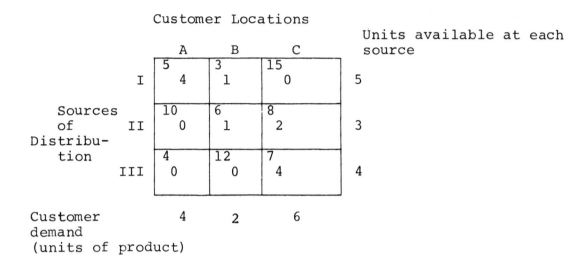

Figure 7-3

The cost of this preliminary solution to the problem is computed as follows:

Shipping route	Number of units	Unit cost	Total cost
I-A	4	$5	$20
I-B	1	3	3
II-B	1	6	6
II-B	2	8	16
III-C	4	7	28
Total shipping cost			$73

Alternative shipping routes are now evaluated to determine whether or not costs can be reduced by substituting some other shipping route for the one selected in the preliminary solution. The opportunity cost of selecting a given route, that is, the cost attached to an alternate shipping plan, is entered in the lower right-hand corner of the unused box. For boxes already in the solution, the cost per unit is repeated in the lower right-hand corner of the box.

The array is given in Figure 7-4 with the opportunity costs filled in.

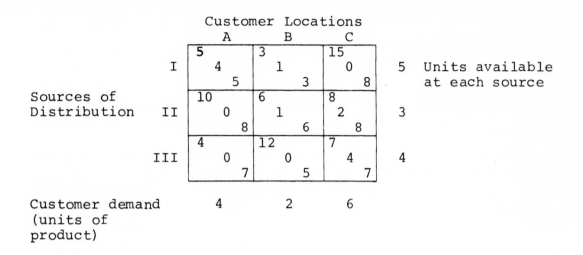

Figure 7-4

The opportunity costs have been computed as shown below. Route I-C, for example, has not been selected. If it were selected, costs per unit would be increased or decreased by a change in the shipping routes.

Costs would be decreased by not shipping over routes I-A and III-C so that a unit could be shipped on route I-C. Costs, however, would be increased by shipping another unit by route III-A to make up for the decrease in a unit that would otherwise be shipped by III-C.

Decreased cost:	
Deleted routes	*Cost reduction per unit*
I-A	$ 5
III-C	7
	$12

Increased cost:	
Added route	*Cost increase per unit*
III-A	$ 4

The net effect would be to reduce costs by $8.

Obviously it won't pay to increase costs by $15 a unit by selecting route I-C if costs can only be reduced by $8 a unit on other routes.

Another alternative may be selected, but it offers even less advantage.

Decreased cost:	*Cost reduction per unit*
I-B	$ 3
II-C	8
	$11

Increased cost:	*Cost increase per unit*
II-B	6

The net effect would be to reduce costs by only $5. In evaluating alternatives, always select the best alternate plan.

Other unused routes are evaluated in the same way; that is, by computing the cost effect of using alternative routes so that the excluded route can be included.

	Deleted routes	*Added routes*	*Cost effect per unit (decrease)*
Route II-A			
	I-A		($ 5)
	II-B		(6)
		I-B	3
Net effect per unit			($ 8)
Route III-A			
	I-A		($ 5)
	II-B		(6)
	III-C		(7)
		I-B	3
		II-C	8
Net effect per unit			($ 7)
Route III-B			
	II-B		($ 6)
	III-C		(7)
		II-C	8
Net effect per unit			$ 5

Costs can be reduced by some other shipping arrangement if the opportunity cost of using a route is larger than the incurred cost to ship by that route. In seeking a solution, start with the route where the cost advantage is largest. In the illustration given, only one excluded route offers any cost advantage. If route III-A is selected, the cost will be increased by $4 a unit by shipping over that route, but there is a net cost saving of $7 a unit by adding and deleting other shipping routes.

The revised solution is given in Figure 7-5.

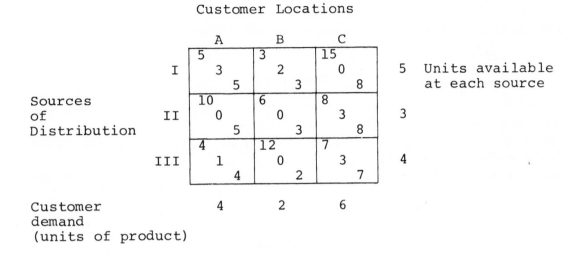

Figure 7-5

The cost of the revised shipping arrangement is computed as follows:

Shipping route	Number of units	Unit cost	Total cost
I-A	3	$ 5	$ 15
I-B	2	3	6
II-C	3	8	24
III-A	1	4	4
III-C	3	7	21
Total shipping cost			$ 70

This solution is the minimum cost solution. Note that the opportunity cost identified with each excluded route is now less than the cost to ship by that route. This means that no further improvements can be made by an alteration of the plan.

Computer Solutions

The illustration is very simple, and yet there were several alternatives to be tested. In practice there may be many alternatives available, and the optimum solution will be the result of many trials. The testing procedure is relatively simple, but it is tedious. This type of problem can be handled conveniently by a computer program that tests various routes and continues the testing procedure until the best solution is found.

Essentially the linear programming problem is a break-even problem. A test is made at each step toward the final solution to determine whether or not costs can be reduced by substituting one variable for another—in this case one shipping route for another. The essential idea may be expressed as follows:

Cost of selecting an alternative $<$ Cost of present plan

If it costs less to substitute the alternative, the alternative should be selected. On the other hand, if the alternative costs more, the present plan is better.

Cost of selecting an alternative $>$ Cost of present plan.

SUMMARY

Profits are improved by controlling not only the production costs but also the costs of selling and distribution. Often costs in the selling area are not given proper attention. A reluctance to examine these costs may arise from a fear that any changes in the methods of advertising and sales promotion may reduce sales volume. Also the human factor is more critical in dealing with customers, and it is difficult to measure all factors in quantitative terms.

Closer examination of some of the sales problems, however, may reveal that measurements can be made in many circumstances—at least, approximate measurements that can help in defining the essential problem and may be a step toward a solution. A break-even approach when used appropriately will help to show how the sales function can be carried out more effectively with the least possible cost.

8

Selecting the
Most Lucrative Product Lines

Should a new product line be added, or should an old one be discontinued? This question will arise at one time or another in making plans for the future. Perhaps an older product line that was once successful is losing customer appeal because of changes in the social environment, improvements in technology, or changes in styles. The product line, instead of contributing to the total operation, may be acting as a brake by reducing total profits. Careful study of the situation may indicate that the product line should be discontinued. There will also be opportunities to add new product lines, and it may be possible to add these lines without expanding facilities.

In many cases specialized machinery and equipment must be acquired, and perhaps additional building space must be provided before a new product can be produced. There will also be situations where a product line can be added to absorb idle capacity, and it will be possible to produce this product with the facilities that are available. In this chapter it is assumed that a product line can be added with no additional investment. If additional investment is required, the product-line decision becomes a capital investment decision, which will be dealt with in Chapter 12.

THE RELEVANT COSTS

Product-line decisions are break-even decisions. Can a new product line under consideration bring in enough revenue to cover its own costs and contribute to the total operation, and can it contribute more than any other available alternative? Or can a product line that is presently being produced cover its own costs and contribute more than some other line that can be substituted in its place? In order to make a decision, both the revenues and costs that are identified with the line must be considered. Costs must be examined carefully to determine whether or not they will be affected by the decision, and if affected to what extent.

Differential Costs

The changes in costs that can be expected from the addition or the deletion of a product line are the relevant costs. The costs that change may be either variable costs or fixed costs. The distinction between variable and fixed costs is based on cost behavior in relation to changes in the hours of activity or changes in the quantity of product produced. In this chapter the cost behavior concept is expanded to distinguish between costs that change and costs that do not change as a result of *any* decision that is to be made, and both the variable and the fixed costs can be changed by a decision.

In decision making, alternatives are compared. It is the difference in revenue and the difference in costs (both variable and fixed) between one alternative and another that are relevant to the decision.

Increases or decreases in costs, whether variable or fixed, are generally called *differential costs.* The increases in cost, either variable or fixed, are more specifically referred to as *incremental costs.* The decreases in cost, either variable or fixed, are more specifically referred to as *decremental costs.*

A distinction between variable and fixed costs is very important in cost control and in making decisions with respect to changes in sales volume, selling prices, and costs within a given range of productive capacity and with given product lines. However, when a decision is to be made as to whether or not a product line or a project is to be undertaken or discontinued, attention is focused on the changes in *all* costs that can be expected as a result of this decision.

Sunk Costs

A cost that has already been incurred is called a *sunk cost.* Costs incurred in the past are not relevant in decision making. What is past is past, and the future is still to come. This is the attitude that must be accepted in decision making, because decision making looks forward into the future and not back into the past. An expenditure, for example, of $5,000 for a piece of equipment that did not live up to expectations may now be recognized as poor judgment, but poor judgment in the past should not be allowed to influence decisions bearing on the future. The cost of this equipment may be written off as depreciation if the equipment is used; if the equipment is sold, the cost less accumulated depreciation to date will be matched against the amount received from the sale in determining any gain or loss. The cost of the equipment, once incurred, cannot be changed. If a decision is to be made as to whether the equipment should be used in operations or sold, forget the equipment cost and compare the present value of the future expected net returns from operation with the proceeds from an immediate sale. Look to the future, don't dwell on the past.

The sunk cost concept may be expanded even further to include not only costs already incurred but costs that will be incurred in the future regardless of the decision made. Costs that will be incurred no matter how the decision goes can be called sunk costs with respect to that decision. For example, either Product X will be added or Product Y will be added to the product lines. In either case, assume that property taxes will amount to $1,200 a year. Property taxes will not influence the decision one way or the other, and even though they are still to be incurred, they can be considered sunk costs with respect to the product-line decision.

A BREAK-EVEN PRESENTATION

The break-even point or the point of indifference on a product-line decision may be set forth in equation form.

Additional revenue = Additional variable cost + Additional fixed cost. (Add a product line.)

Reduced revenue = Reduced variable cost + Reduced fixed cost. (Drop a product line.)

Or the equations may be restated as follows:

$$\text{Incremental revenue} = \text{Incremental cost} \quad \text{(Add a product line.)}$$

or

$$\text{Decremental revenue} = \text{Decremental cost} \quad \text{(Drop a product line.)}$$

The decision is in favor of adding a new product line if

$$\text{Incremental revenue} > \text{Incremental cost.}$$

It is unfavorable if

$$\text{Incremental revenue} < \text{Incremental cost.}$$

A product line should be dropped, everything else being equal, if

$$\text{Decremental revenue} < \text{Decremental cost.}$$

On the other hand, a product line should be retained if

$$\text{Decremental revenue} > \text{Decremental cost.}$$

The same result can be obtained from a tabular form of presentation. Assume that a new product line is expected to add $20,000 to revenue each year with additional variable costs of $12,000 and additional fixed costs of $5,000. The factors bearing on the decision may be assembled as follows:

Incremental revenue	$20,000
Incremental variable costs	12,000
Incremental contribution margin	$ 8,000
Incremental fixed cost	5,000
Net advantage of new product line	$ 3,000

IDENTIFICATION OF THE RELEVANT COSTS

Unfortunately it is not possible to set forth a list of costs that will always change when product lines are added or deleted. Each situation will be different. In one case, for example, it may be possible to reduce supervisory salaries by dropping a product line, while in another case the supervisory salaries may not be changed. It may be necessary to lay off supervisors in one case, while in another it may be possible to transfer them to a different area of operations. Each situation has to be examined separately to determine the cost effect.

The general rule to follow is to consider all costs that may be affected by the decision. For the costs that can be expected to change, determine the amount of the increase or decrease. In practice it may not always be easy to identify the costs that change and to measure the extent of the changes. The impact of a change may extend beyond the area of manufacturing into sales and administration. For example, a new product line may present problems in packaging and shipping with increased costs, or the customer accounting problem may be different with the result being higher costs of administration. In making an evaluation of this sort, every possible effect must be considered; otherwise the decision may be incorrect.

THE ADDITION OF A PRODUCT LINE

If a new product line is to be added, there are several factors that must be considered. It is assumed, of course, that the company has the capacity available for the production and sale of this line and that it has the technical competence required to handle it. In addition, does the product line fit into the existing family of products, or is it entirely different? A product line that helps to round out the family of product lines may be favored to an extent because it not only can contribute profits itself but may help to bolster sales of the related lines. What type of new product is under consideration? Perhaps there is a short-run idle capacity problem, and a relatively low-profit line may be accepted on a temporary basis until there is an improvement in regular operations. Or the objective may be to add a line on a permanent basis.

After the problem itself has been defined, it will be possible to consider the expected economic effects. For example, assume that a new product line is under study and that it is anticipated that this line if accepted will be accepted on a permanent basis. Each year the new line is expected to add $170,000 to revenue. The additional costs to produce and sell this product line each year are listed below.

	Increases (incremental costs)
Variable manufacturing costs:	
Direct materials	$ 46,000
Direct labor	34,000
Indirect materials and supplies	18,000
Fixed manufacturing costs:	
Supervisory salaries	30,000
Heat and light	2,000
Insurance and taxes	1,500
Selling and administrative costs:	
Advertising	4,000
Sales commissions	17,000
Office supplies	500
Office salaries	8,000
Total incremental costs	$161,000

There may be circumstances in which costs can be reduced by the decision, in which case the estimated *net* increase in costs will be compared with the estimated increase in revenue.

In this example, it was assumed that costs could not be reduced. The new product line is acceptable on an economic basis, but it may not be the most acceptable alternative available.

$$\begin{array}{ccc} \textit{Incremental revenue} & & \textit{Incremental cost} \\ \$170,000 & > & \$161,000. \end{array}$$

A $9,000 advantage can be identified with this product line, and this advantage becomes the opportunity cost of any other alternative that is available.

For example, suppose that another alternative can be expected to add $130,000 to revenue and to add $90,000 to cost each year. This line would then be favored.

$$\begin{array}{cccccc} & & & & \textit{Opportunity cost} \\ & & & & \textit{(Advantage of the} \\ \textit{Incremental revenue} & & \textit{Incremental cost} & & \textit{next best alternative)} \\ \$130,000 & > & \$90,000 & + & \$9,000 \end{array}$$

The net advantage is computed below.

$$\begin{array}{ccccccc} \textit{Net advantage} & & \textit{Incremental revenue} & & \textit{Incremental cost} & & \textit{Opportunity cost} \\ \$31,000 & = & \$130,000 & - & (\$90,000 & + & \$9,000) \end{array}$$

The net advantage to be derived from this product line now becomes the opportunity cost of any other alternative. Assuming that there are no other factors to complicate the decision, the best alternative should be selected.

If a product line is to be accepted on a temporary basis to utilize excess capacity, it may not be possible to examine many alternatives. Less profitable alternatives may be accepted, and properly so, if a decision must be made quickly. After all, it is better to make some profit instead of waiting for the best alternative to appear. However, this does not mean that a decision should be made in haste before obtaining all of the relevant facts. Nor does it mean that a weak product line that is accepted on a temporary basis should be permitted to remain until it becomes a permanent part of the product line structure.

In some cases the decision to accept or to reject a product line cannot be made on the basis of the results for any one year. It may take time to develop profit potential, and costs may exceed revenues in the early years. Then in later years the product will develop momentum and yield profits. An evaluation of a product that is expected to develop over the years is more difficult because of the long time interval and future uncertainty. A decision that involves a comparison of amounts spread over future time periods is a capital investment decision even though it does not involve an investment in tangible machinery, equipment, or fixtures.

This particular type of capital investment decision is also a product-line decision that will be encountered frequently. In making a comparison of revenues and costs, the future revenues and costs must be restated on a present value basis. A comparison of future dollar amounts with present dollar amounts is valid only if the dollars are all on the same time basis. The future dollar amounts should be placed on a present value basis; this can be done by discounting these future amounts at the rate of return that the company can expect from its investments.

Assume, for example, that a company has estimated that a new product line will yield returns over a period of five years and has estimated annual incremental revenues and incremental costs as follows:

Year	Incremental revenue	Incremental cost	Incremental profit (loss)
1	$ 30,000	$ 50,000	($ 20,000)
2	50,000	40,000	10,000
3	80,000	50,000	30,000
4	110,000	60,000	50,000
5	100,000	60,000	40,000

The company expects a rate of return on its investments of 20 percent and uses this rate to discount future amounts to a present value. The incremental profits and losses are discounted as shown below.

Year	Incremental profit (loss)	Present value of $1, 20%	Present value of incremental profit (loss)
1	($20,000)	.833	($16,666)
2	10,000	.694	6,940
3	30,000	.579	17,370
4	50,000	.482	24,100
5	40,000	.402	16,080
	Present value of estimated profits		$47,824

This product line meets the minimum rate-of-return requirement in the long run. If a decision were made on the basis of the first year of operation or even the first two years, the product line would be rejected. And this would be the incorrect decision if no better alternative were available.

Admittedly the returns from the sale of products do not appear precisely at the end of each year but instead flow in regularly or irregularly during the year. A continuous discount rate may be used if desired, but this degree of precision is not required in most cases. The objective is to select the best product line alternative and not to compute a precise rate of return. If the flow of returns from all alternatives during each year can be expected to follow the same pattern, the annual discount rate will be sufficient.

Some product lines may not have limited useful lives but may be expected to produce returns indefinitely. Even so, very few product lines will produce returns indefinitely without modifications. For all practical purposes, little can be gained by estimating and discounting returns for more than ten years into the future. Furthermore, the discounted returns in distant years will have little effect on the results.

THE ELIMINATION OF A PRODUCT LINE

The same type of analysis used for the selection of a new product line can be used in deciding whether or not a product line should be eliminated. Only the line of direction is different. In place of additional revenue and additional cost, there will be reduced revenue and reduced cost. And if the reduction in cost exceeds the reduction in revenue, the product line should be discontinued, assuming no other relevant factors.

An income statement showing the results by product lines is given below.

Income Statement
For the year, 19xx

	Total	A	B	C	D
			Product Lines		
Net sales	$512,000	$180,700	$125,100	$ 85,800	$120,400
Cost of goods sold	271,100	80,500	80,600	55,100	54,900
Store supplies	16,000	3,200	3,100	5,300	4,400
Shipping supplies	48,300	11,100	18,300	9,700	9,200
Sales salaries	61,000	15,900	19,600	11,200	14,300
Supervisory salaries	43,000	14,000	7,000	12,000	10,000
Advertising	24,000	7,600	8,700	3,600	4,100
Heat and light	9,000	2,200	2,100	2,700	2,000
Taxes and insurance	6,500	1,700	1,300	1,800	1,700
Repairs and maintenance	10,000	2,800	2,000	2,800	2,400
Depreciation	16,700	4,200	3,800	4,700	4,000
Total expenses	$505,600	$143,200	$146,500	$108,900	$107,000
Net income (loss)	$ 6,400	$ 37,500	($ 21,400)	($ 23,100)	$ 13,400

The net income on the total operation is relatively low when compared with sales revenue, and it may seem that it can be increased from $6,400 to $50,900 by eliminating products B and C. With the losing product lines removed, it would appear that the losses associated with these lines of $44,500 ($21,400 + $23,100) can also be removed. Will the elimination of these lines really increase profits?

Before making any decision, more information is needed. Will the elimination of a product line reduce costs by more than the reduction of revenue from the product line? This is the heart of the problem, a comparison of the effect on revenue with the effect on cost. Many costs will still be incurred even after the product line is eliminated, while other costs will be reduced. The costs that will be incurred anyway will only have to be absorbed by the other product lines if the product line is dropped.

In the illustration assume that the following costs can be eliminated if the product line is discontinued:

> Cost of goods sold
> Shipping supplies
> Sales salaries
> Advertising

All of the other costs have been allocated to the product lines and will be incurred if any product lines are handled. If one line is discontinued, the costs that have been allocated to that line will have to be reallocated to the other lines. These costs are sunk costs with respect to the product-line decision.

An income statement with costs classified as to whether or not they can be eliminated by an elimination of the product line will reveal the product lines that cannot bring in enough revenue to cover their own costs. If there are no complicating factors, a product line that cannot produce enough revenue to cover its own costs should be eliminated. However, a product line showing a net loss may still produce more than enough revenue to cover its own costs. If a product contributes to the overall operation it should be retained, provided, of course, that better opportunities are not available. Care must be exercised in making decisions to retain product lines that contribute little to the total operation. Without intending to do so, management may end up with many product lines that yield poor contribution margins.

The costs that can be eliminated with the elimination of a product line are labeled as escapable costs on the income statement given below. The costs that will not be affected by the product-line decision are labeled as inescapable costs.

Income Statement
For the year, 19xx

	Total	A	B	C	D
Net sales	$512,000	$180,700	$125,100	$85,800	$120,400
Escapable costs:					
Cost of goods sold	$271,100	$ 80,500	$ 80,600	$55,100	$ 54,900
Shipping supplies	48,300	11,100	18,300	9,700	9,200
Sales salaries	61,000	15,900	19,600	11,200	14,300
Advertising	24,000	7,600	8,700	3,600	4,100
Total escapable costs	$404,400	$115,100	$127,200	$79,600	$ 82,500
Margin over escapable costs	$107,600	$ 65,600	($ 2,100)	$ 6,200	$ 37,900
Inescapable costs:					
Store supplies	$ 16,000				
Supervisory salaries	43,000				
Heat and light	9,000				
Taxes and insurance	6,500				
Repairs and maintenance	10,000				
Depreciation	16,700				
Total inescapable costs	$101,200				
Net income (loss)	$ 6,400				

This statement clearly shows that Product B should be eliminated and that Product C should be retained. If Product B is discontinued, costs will be reduced by more than the loss of revenue from the sale of the product, and the total profit can be increased by $2,100. Product C, on the other hand, cannot cover its share of the allocated cost, but it does contribute $6,200 to the total operation. If Product C were discontinued, the contribution of $6,200 to the recovery of the inescapable costs would be lost and the total profit would be reduced to $200 ($6,400–$6,200).

A BREAK-EVEN APPROACH

A solution to this type of problem can be obtained much more easily by the break-even approach. Determine the revenue derived from each line and compare it with the costs that can be eliminated by elimination of the product line. If the costs exceed the revenue, the line should be eliminated; otherwise, the line should be retained.

Product B

Decreased revenue		Decreased cost
$125,100	<	$127,200

Drop Product B.

Product C

Decreased revenue		Decreased cost
$85,800	>	$79,600

Retain Product C.

The effect on the total profit can be seen by returning to the final net income shown on the income statement and adjusting it by the decreases in revenue and cost that can be expected if a product line is discontinued.

Effect of eliminating Product B:

Net income	$ 6,400
Add decreased cost	127,200
	$133,600
Deduct decreased revenue	125,100
Net income without Product B	$ 8,500

Effect of eliminating Product C:

Net income	$ 6,400
Add decreased cost	79,600
	$ 86,000
Deduct decreased revenue	85,800
Net income without Product C	$ 200

OTHER FACTORS IN THE PROBLEM

The product-line decision as presented appears to present no great problem once the escapable costs are identified. This part of the analysis *is* relatively simple, but it may be only the beginning of the analytical process.

It has been assumed that the income statement used in the illustration is typical of the operation. If the revenues or costs associated with the product lines are abnormally high or low in that particular year, a valid decision cannot be made. The costs associated with Product B (the escapable costs), for example, may have been unusually high on this income statement. That is, for some reason or other, the escapable costs associated with Product B may have been abnormally high during the year. Perhaps with better cost control in the future, the costs can be reduced substantially. If this is true, a decision to eliminate Product B may be incorrect.

The analysis should be extended beyond the narrow confines of the product lines themselves. Must Product B be retained in order to sell Product A? If so, Product B and Product A must be evaluated together. The loss on Product B may have to be accepted if the company is to sell Product A.

Perhaps Product C should be eliminated even though it contributes to the operation. Can the resources used to support Product C be used to better advantage to support an expansion of sales for Products A or D? Or can a better product line be substituted for Product C? If another product line is to replace Product C, it must contribute more than $6,200 to the total operation. Stated in another way, the contribution of $6,200 from Product C becomes the opportunity cost of any other line that may be substituted in its place.

Any product line, for that matter, may be challenged by a line that promises a greater profit contribution. And the profit contribution should be evaluated on a long-range basis. An attempt to gain a short-run advantage may not be profitable in the long run. For example, a product may be quite profitable as a novelty but will not have any lasting effect on profits. It may be poor policy to replace a stable line that produces regular profits over the years with a high-profit item that won't hold up.

Store and plant capacity are limited. It is important that the available facilities be used to the best advantage in earning profits for the company. Essentially, this is a problem of optimization of resources. In the preceding chapter, a simple illustration was given to show how linear programming can be used to select the most economical shipping routes. Alternatives were compared, and less costly alternatives were substituted until no better alternatives could be found. Similarly, this approach may be used to optimize the use of time or space. As stated before, linear programming is a form of break-even analysis that compares one alternative with another, substitutes when a better alternative is available, and continues this process until there are no better alternatives.

SUMMARY

In selecting product lines, the central point is to distinguish between revenues and costs that will be changed by the decision and revenues and costs that will not be affected. A product line that will add more to revenue than it adds to cost may be an acceptable addition to the total operation. However, with limited facilities, management must select the best alternative and will compare product-line candidates on the basis of their contributions to profits.

A product line may be discontinued if elimination of that line will reduce costs by more than it will reduce revenues. Other factors must be considered before making a final judgment. Perhaps there is a relationship among the product lines; and a losing product line may be retained because it indirectly produces profits by increasing the sales of a profitable line.

9

Determining Differential
Market Prices

Inasmuch as profits depend upon both revenues and costs, both sides of the profit structure deserve equal attention. Perhaps costs are frequently given more attention because of the difficulty of identifying them with a product or because they can ordinarily be controlled more readily by management. Revenues on the other hand depend upon prices, and prices may be fixed by the conditions of the market place, custom, and the actions of competitors. It is true, of course, that costs may also be established by outside influences that lie beyond the control of management.

Even with outside influences, however, there is usually some degree of freedom in setting prices. There may be product lines that are not directly affected by the actions of competitors, or some distinctive features may differentiate a product from similar products on the market. Aside from the problem of establishing regular prices, there is the additional problem of deciding when prices should be increased or decreased and to what extent. There is also the problem of setting prices for different market situations.

PRICING THE NEW PRODUCT

An entirely new type of product is often introduced on the market at a premium price, and when the product becomes established, the price will be reduced. Style-conscious customers are often willing to pay more in order to be the first ones to have a new type of product. After this market has been satisfied, the price will have to be reduced to obtain a mass market. Examples of price distinctions of this type are evident in women's fashions, in the introduction of color television, and in various situations involving product innovations. In marketing, the premium price is called a *skimming price.*

The skimming price may not always bring in extra profits. In fact, the initial price may have to be established at a high level to recover the high costs of development and initial production. As the production process becomes routine, both the costs and the prices can be reduced. The customer who is willing to pay the higher price performs a useful service in that he encourages product innovation. The company, for its part, must be able to estimate how much the elite customer will be willing to pay and to determine the point where this demand has been satisfied. The timing of a change in price is another variation of break-even analysis. The break-even point or point of price change is the point at which the estimated profits with a skimming price are equal to the estimated profits with a reduced or regular price. If competition is a factor, however, it may be necessary to sacrifice some of the profits from a skimming price in order to establish an early position in the mass market.

Estimated profits with a skimming price = Estimated profits with a regular price.

In marketing a new product, the market situation must be studied carefully. The skimming price concept may be useful in some cases, and detrimental in others. Under certain conditions, a skimming price may help to recover high initial development costs and produce higher profits. Ordinarily this will be true when substitutes cannot be obtained from competitors and when the product has a style appeal. In some cases, however, an unusually high price may drive off potential customers and kill off a promising new product line. In making this type of pricing decision, consideration must be given to the attitudes of the potential customers, the nature of the product, customs within the industry, and general economic conditions.

SEASONAL PRICE VARIATIONS

Some types of merchandise are seasonal, or there may be model changes each year. During the season, this merchandise will be offered for sale at regular prices; near the end of the season or before the model changes, prices will be reduced to clear out the old stock. A large part of the total profit for the year may be derived from sales at the regular prices with the special year-end sales contributing additional profits. The special year-end sale may be looked upon as a clearance sale to eliminate old stock in preparation for the new season. In other cases, perhaps, the special sale may be a regular feature that will contribute a significant amount to total profits.

The break-even type of analysis becomes more complicated with price differences during the year. Demand will have to be predicted under each price condition, and some consideration must be given to the possibility that the total demand may shift from the higher priced market to the lower priced market. If it is generally known that a special sale is held each year, customers may wait for the sale and buy at lower prices. The firm may be putting forth more effort by holding a special sale but may be earning less than it would otherwise.

When customers can time their purchases to obtain more favorable prices, the firm must be careful not to encourage a migration of regular customers to the special sales. This can be accomplished to some extent by restricting the period of time for the sale and by granting only modest price concessions. If old stock must be cleared out, a clearance sale may be held at the completion of the special sale. Customers are not as likely to wait for the clearance sale because it will be held only if there is stock remaining after the special sale. If a customer waits too long, he may not be able to buy at a reduced price.

An Illustration of Special Sales Prices

Regardless of the sales strategy employed, it will be necessary to estimate the effect on profits. Suppose, for example, that a certain item of merchandise is priced at $20 and that no price concessions are granted. Ordinarily, 80,000 units of this product are sold each year. The variable cost per unit is $12, and the total fixed cost for the year is $400,000. The profit for the year of $240,000 is shown on the P/V Graph given in Figure 9-1.

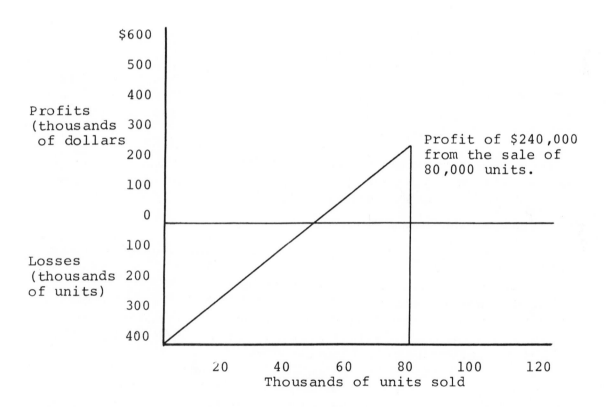

Figure 9-1

Assume now that the firm hopes to stimulate additional sales volume and to clear out old stock by having a year-end sale. The price is reduced from $20 to $15, and if regular sales can be maintained, profits will be increased if additional units can be sold at any price in excess of the unit variable cost of $12.

The increased profits, however, did not materialize as expected even though total sales volume increased from 80,000 to 90,000 units. In anticipation of the sale regular customers delayed making purchases, and sales were distributed as follows:

60,000 units sold at $20 per unit.
30,000 units sold at $15 per unit.

Sales of 20,000 units at the regular price were shifted to the special sale. This in itself reduces profits by $100,000. The contribution margin per unit at the regular price is $8 ($20 selling price minus $12 unit variable cost). At the reduced price, the contribution margin per unit is $3 ($15 selling price minus $12 unit variable cost). Hence, the contribution margin is reduced on a unit basis by $5 and by $100,000 in total with a shift of 20,000 units to the special sale. The increase in sales volume of 10,000 units adds $30,000 to profits (10,000 units x $3).

The net result is a reduction in total profits from $240,000 to $170,000, a reduction of $70,000.

Reduced contribution margin caused by a shift of 20,000 units to the special sale	$100,000
Less increased contribution margin from a 10,000-unit increase in sales volume	30,000
Net reduction in profits	$ 70,000

The profit with the special sale is shown on the P/V graph in Figure 9-2. The profit as shown before at $240,000 is depicted again on this graph by dotted lines. Note how the profit line flattens out after the price is reduced.

Pricing Problems with Seasonal Merchandise

In the illustration given, the special sale at a reduced price increased sales volume but not profits. Too many sales that could have been made at the regular price were made at the lower price as a result of customers waiting for the special sale.

The decision as to whether or not the price should be reduced at the end of a season is a version of the general problem of whether or not prices should be reduced to increase sales volume and profits. In either case, the effect of changes in sales volume must be combined with the effect of a reduced selling price.

If a clearance sale must be held to clear out old merchandise, the firm may have to accept whatever it can get from leftover merchandise and at the same time accept the risk that customers may wait for the reduced prices. Perhaps the problem can be relieved somewhat by holding surplus stock to a minimum, which may be accomplished by estimating demand more closely. The decision to order certain quantities of perishable products and services for the customers was discussed in Chapter 7.

BRAND AND OFF-BRAND MERCHANDISE

A similar problem of pricing arises when a manufacturer sells a well-known product under its brand label at a regular price and sells virtually the same line of product

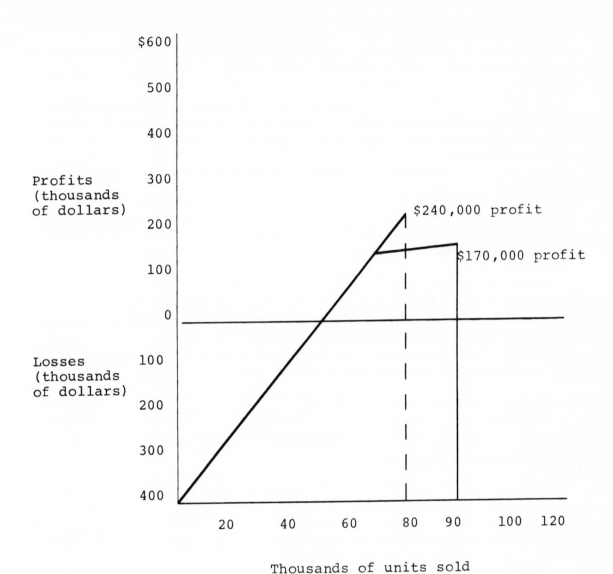

Profits
(thousands
of dollars)

$240,000 profit

$170,000 profit

Losses
(thousands
of dollars)

Thousands of units sold

Figure 9-2

through discount chains or other outlets at a lower price under a different brand label. The double market situation has an advantage in allowing a company to enter a lower priced market while at the same time retaining its hold on the quality market. However, if the customers recognize that there is a two-price market for the same goods, they will shift over to the lower priced market and total profits may be lower.

There may be a greater risk that a customer will shift from a standard product to an off-brand product than from a regular price to a special price. Special sales prices are not definite, and a customer cannot always be sure of price concessions at the end of a season. With virtually the same product being sold under different labels, there is little if any insulation between the markets. Eventually, the customers will learn that the products are the same and will tend to buy in the lower priced market.

Two markets can be created, however, by giving special services and warranties with branded merchandise that are not available on the off-brand products. These distinctive features may appeal to a certain class of customer who will be willing to pay more to obtain them. If these differences are recognized by the customer, he will be less likely to switch to the lower priced market, assuming, of course, that he accepts the value of these services as being approximately equal to the price differential.

A PHYSICAL SEPARATION OF MARKETS

Distances between regions and countries may also help to create separate markets. For example, a product may be sold in the domestic market for one price and at another price in a foreign market. If there is a true separation of markets, customers will not shift from one market to the other. In effect, it is like selling different product lines in one market.

Assume, for example, that a certain product line with a unit variable manufactured cost of $10 is sold in the domestic market for $30 a unit and in a foreign market at a price of $20 a unit. Shipping and delivery costs amount to $2 a unit in the domestic market and $5 a unit in the foreign market. Total fixed costs for the year are estimated at $600,000. The company plans to sell 80,000 units in the domestic market next year, and 30,000 units in the foreign market. Profits are anticipated as follows:

	Total	Domestic	Foreign
Units sold	110,000	80,000	30,000
Sales	$3,000,000	$2,400,000	$600,000
Variable costs:			
Manufacturing	$1,100,000	$ 800,000	$300,000
Shipping and delivery	310,000	160,000	150,000
Total variable costs	$1,410,000	$ 960,000	$450,000
Contribution margin	$1,590,000	$1,440,000	$150,000
Fixed costs	600,000		
Net income	$ 990,000		

The foreign market contributes $150,000 to the total operation and brings in additional profits that would not be realized from domestic operations alone. As a general rule it can be stated that a product line can be sold at a price in excess of its variable costs, it will contribute profits to the total operation, provided, of course, that it sells in sufficient volume to cover more than its own additional fixed costs. This rule, while generally true, has exceptions.

In the example given, sales in the foreign market should produce additional profits. The product is sold for $20 a unit, the variable costs amount to $15 a unit, and there are no additional fixed costs. Each unit then can be expected to contribute $5 to total profits.

In this situation, however, there is another very significant break-even point. And this break-even point is as important as the conventional break-even point computed from selling prices, variable costs, and fixed costs. Additional profits may not be derived from a foreign market if prices have not been established properly in each market. In fact, the total profits may be reduced. Perhaps the product may be purchased at a favorable price in the foreign market and shipped back to the domestic market for resale at a price that is lower than the established domestic price. As a result, foreign sales may be increased at the expense of domestic sales. If it costs $5 to ship each unit to the foreign market, it may cost $5, or even less, to return the unit to the domestic market.

An enterprising individual may purchase the product in a foreign country, ship it back to the domestic market, and resell it below the established domestic price and realize a profit on his operation. In the example given, this could happen even assuming that the buyer must absorb the domestic shipping costs of $2 a unit.

Domestic selling price		$30
Cost to an outsider:		
Cost to buy in the foreign market	$20	
Cost to ship to the domestic market	5	
Cost to deliver in the domestic market	2	27
Advantage to outsider		$ 3

Assume now that someone does take advantage of the price spread. The sales in the domestic market are reduced to 20,000 units and are increased to 90,000 units in the foreign market. Profits will then be as follows:

	Total	Domestic	Foreign
Units sold	110,000	20,000	90,000
Sales	$1,400,000	$600,000	$1,800,000
Variable costs:			
Manufacturing	$1,100,000	$200,000	$ 900,000
Shipping and delivery costs	490,000	40,000	$ 450,000
Total variable costs	$1,590,000	$240,000	$1,350,000
Contribution margin	$ 810,000	$360,000	$ 450,000
Fixed costs	600,000		
Net income	$ 210,000		

The profits will be considerably lower with a shift to the foreign market. Figuratively speaking, someone left the gate open, and the profits went down the road! Prices should be established in each market so that transfers between markets will not be profitable to outsiders. For example, in this case, with a selling price of $23 in the foreign market, there will be no profit in returning units to the domestic market.

Domestic selling price		$30
Cost to an outsider:		
Cost to buy in the foreign market	$23	
Cost to ship to the domestic market	5	
Cost to deliver in the domestic market	2	30
Break-even point		-0-

In establishing prices for different markets, management must see that the price differential is small enough to protect the higher priced market. In this example, the domestic price must be equal to or less than the cost to buy the product in a foreign market plus the cost that will be incurred by the buyer to return the product to the domestic market and to deliver it to his domestic customer. This can be expressed in equation form as follows:

Domestic price	$\leq$	Foreign price plus minimum cost of shipment to domestic market and cost to deliver to a domestic customer.

An alternate solution working with differential prices will give the same results.

Price differential between markets	$\leq$	Minimum cost to ship to the higher priced market and to deliver to the customers.

In computing the maximum price spread, the shipping and delivery costs are not necessarily the costs that would be incurred by the manufacturer. An outsider may be able to reduce these costs considerably, and the costs estimated for the outsider are the relevant costs in establishing a price differential.

Price differences between markets can be greater if there are real barriers between the markets. For example, if taxes are levied on imports, it will be more expensive to return goods to the domestic market for sale; as a result, an outsider will find it more difficult to make a profit by working within the price spread. The import taxes are handled in the equation as an additional cost to the outsider, assuming, of course, that the outsider is operating within the law.

CONTRACT BIDS

The contract bid is a specialized type of price differentiation. Products may ordinarily be sold at established prices on a regular commercial market with contract bids being an exception to the general rule. Often special prices are offered on large orders or bids are made on contracts in order to absorb idle capacity and to earn some additional profit. In effect, the contract bid is a price concession much like the price concessions granted on special sales or on clearance sales.

Many firms, because of the nature of their business, will perform most of their work on a contract basis. The contract then is the normal basis for business operation, and it is obvious that the success or failure of the firm depends upon the ability of management to estimate costs accurately, to hold costs to a minimum, to bid low enough to receive the contract awards, and to make reasonable profits on the total investment. Anyone who has ever attempted to set a bid price knows that this is a very difficult task requiring a great deal of knowledge, skill, and courage.

Many of the points discussed in this chapter will apply both to the firms that operate occasionally on a contract basis and to those that operate regularly on a contract basis. Emphasis, however, will be placed upon the problems of the occasional contractor. In his case, the contract is a special situation with a price differential. The regular contractor is not working with a special situation. To him, the contract is normal.

Identification of Differential Costs

Estimates must be made of the increases or decreases in costs that can be expected if the contract is obtained. Some of the costs may be fairly easy to estimate from advertised contract specifications. For example, it may be possible to estimate materials requirements from the specifications; if similar work has been done in the past, labor and overhead increases may also be predicted with some degree of assurance. Even so, questions will arise. Does this contract appear to be typical, or are there pecularities that may cause difficulty? Is there a possibility that some of the work may have to be redone because it doesn't meet specifications? Where are the trouble spots, and how much more will it cost if something goes wrong?

Furthermore, in estimating the costs, attention must be given to the less obvious areas. Costs that are ordinarily fixed may have to be increased if the contract work is done. For example, additional supervisory help may be needed, or there may be increased office salaries because of the extra help required to keep records on the contract work. All cost effects must be considered. It will be too late after the contract is accepted.

The Sunk Costs

Costs that will not be affected by the contract should not be allocated in deciding upon a bid price. Assuming that the contractor accepts the risk and is not protected by a cost plus type of contract, he must consider all costs that will be changed as a result of the contract. Costs that will remain the same whether the contract is accepted or not may be disregarded.

Sunk costs—that is, the costs that will not change because of the contract—typically include building occupancy costs such as depreciation, heat and light, property taxes, and insurance. Plant superintendence and other indirect labor costs may also be sunk costs with respect to the contract. Nothing can be taken for granted, however. Each cost should be considered and not assumed to be a sunk cost merely because it has been one in past decisional situations.

A Closer Look at Sunk Costs

In a decisional situation, it will not always be easy to make a clear distinction between differential costs and sunk costs. A cost may not be increased by accepting a contract, but the contract may exert a pressure upon time and the existing facilities. For example, if a contract is accepted, the plant superintendent may be required to spend some of his time on contract supervision. His salary is not increased because of the contract and is a sunk cost with respect to the decision, yet his time is absorbed if the contract is taken. Should some value be placed on this time in arriving at a bid price?

The answer to this question depends upon the circumstances. If the plant superintendent can delegate some of the supervisory work to others or if he can absorb the contract supervision without neglecting other responsibilities, the contract should not be charged with the value of his time.

On the other hand, pressures placed upon personnel and facilities cannot be overlooked. All too frequently the tendency is to accept one more duty when one is already overburdened. This follows the reasoning that there is always room for one more person on an elevator! The last person to enter may have been the immediate cause of a breakdown, but each person aboard contributed to it. Similarly, a firm can only handle so much work with a given capacity. If the plant superintendent is forced to give less attention to other areas, the cost of this neglect may be looked upon as an additional cost associated with the contract.

Going a step further, it may be appropriate to charge each additional contract with a portion of the *future* cost increases that can be expected from taking on more work. One or two additional contracts may be absorbed by the existing facility, but the third one may make it necessary to hire an assistant superintendent or to expand the physical plant. The third contract should not be charged with the entire cost of the additions. All contracts should bear their share of this cost.

As stated before, a decision of this type depends upon the circumstances. If for some reason the company is anxious to get this contract so that it can develop more business of this sort in the future, some sacrifices may be accepted. Within certain limits, a firm may even accept modest losses on a contract if future benefits can be expected, or short-run contracts may be taken to absorb temporary idle capacity. In these circumstances, the value of time drawn from other activity or the cost of future expansion may be disregarded.

In other circumstances, costs of this nature should be recognized. If there is an appreciable interference with other work because of the contract, the cost should be identified with the contract decision, or if the contract is likely to lead to expansion in the future, the future cost discounted to a present value should be associated with the contract. However, caution should be exercised when including future costs in bid estimates. If too much weight is attached to future costs, attractive current contracts may be lost by overbidding. A zone of tolerance should be established in evaluating the uncertainties of the future.

An Example of a Contract Bid

Assume, for illustration, that a contract is to be awarded for the delivery of 100,000 units of a component that is similar in many respects to a product that is presently being manufactured and sold in the commercial market. The company does not plan to expand in the contract area, but the contract can help to absorb a temporary idle capacity condition.

In deciding upon a bid price, management has made a thorough study of the effect of the contract on costs. Materials requirements have been established, and estimates have been made of the amount of productive labor that will be needed on the contract. Any unusual features of this component have been carefully considered. The variable manufacturing overhead costs tend to increase with direct labor hours, and this has been taken into account along with variations that can be attributed to the contract work itself. Additional supervisory help must be hired, there will also be an increase in indirect labor for increased maintenance work, and part-time help must be hired in the office to handle the accounting records in connection with the contract. Finally, there will be the cost to ship the components to the customer.

The additional costs as estimated are listed below.

Direct materials	$178,500
Direct labor	73,200
Variable manufacturing overhead	46,300
Supervisory salaries	30,000
Other indirect labor cost	25,000
Part-time office salaries	4,000
Shipping costs	8,000
Cost increases identified with the contract	$365,000

The management has also estimated *future* costs that will be incurred if capacity must be expanded at some later date. New machinery will be needed, and more plant space must be provided if the company plans to operate on a larger scale. The share of additional future cost to be assigned to this contract has been estimated on a present value basis at $40,000, using as a present value factor the lowest rate of return that can be accepted on investments of this type. However, in this case, the additional future cost has been disregarded in establishing a bid price. The contract is not expected to become a part of the permanent operation. It is accepted as a temporary device to absorb idle capacity while the demand for the regular market is below normal. If this is the case, situations of this type must not be allowed to creep into the picture on a permanent basis.

The question now arises as to the amount that must be added to the cost estimate for profit. The company will probably not receive the award as low bidder if it includes a normal rate of profit, yet the profit must be reasonably attractive if the work is to be undertaken. A few questions may be asked in an attempt to resolve the profit problem.

How much additional profit can be expected if the facilities are used for some other purpose? For example, if the facilities devoted to the contract can be used in some other way to earn a profit of $20,000, then the opportunity cost of the sacrificed profit of $20,000 becomes a cost of the contract. If, however, there is no other alternative available, this type of problem doesn't arise.

Are the cost estimates reliable or is there some degree of uncertainty? If there is uncertainty, the most probable cost estimate can be used; if there is no basis for prediction, the highest estimate can be used to protect the company against losses.

The temptation to estimate costs on the low side in order to get the contract should be resisted. It is not always an advantage to get the contract. Remember that losses as well as profits can be derived from contracts, and sometimes a contractor may find himself in a situation where he would be better off without the work.

The bid price should be at a point where the company is indifferent as to whether or not it receives the contract. This is the fulcrum or break-even point. Management should take the attitude that if anyone else is willing to do the work at a lower price, let them have it. If the company is awarded the contract, that is also good. The cost estimates are sound, and there is no reason to be concerned about the ability to perform the work and to earn a profit.

In the example given, it is assumed that the turning point is reached at about ten percent. The bid price is set at an even amount of $400,000 or at $4.00 per unit. Admittedly, this allowance for profit is somewhat arbitrary and cannot be calculated precisely by equation. Presumably, management has decided that for the amount of time and money involved, a $35,000 profit or a profit of approximately this amount is minimum. If the company is not particularly anxious for the business because of other opportunities that may be developing, the bid price may be raised to allow a higher profit margin.

SUMMARY

Both revenues and costs are important in profit control. On the revenue side, prices are a very important factor that to some degree can be controlled by the sellers, and one of the problems included in the general pricing problem is the problem of setting prices for different markets. The price spread between markets must not be large enough to encourage customers to shift from the higher priced market to the lower priced market. The maximum price differential between markets separated by physical location can be solved for by a break-even type of analysis, and the amount of the differential should be no greater than the costs to ship the product from the lower cost market to the higher cost market. Contract bidding is a special pricing situation. Ideally the bid price should be at a balancing point where the company is as satisifed with the profit if the contract is awarded as it is to forego the profit if someone else gets the contract.

10

Deciding Whether to Extend
or Contract Operations

Sometimes a company will consider an extension of its operations by producing a part or component used in manufacturing its product lines, or operations may be extended in the other direction by doing more work on the present product lines to put them into a more completed form. The two directions of an extended operation may be visualized as follows:

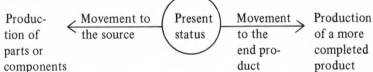

A decision may also be made to contract the scope of operations. For example, if parts are presently being manufactured, a company may decide to discontinue this manufacturing operation and purchase the parts from outside suppliers. Similarly, a decision may be made to discontinue the production of a completed product and to sell a partially completed product to other manufacturers who specialize in the finishing operations.

An extension type of decision differs from an expansion type of decision. Expansion involves an inrecase in volume of production and sales without respect to the particular product lines, but the extension is a move to integrate production either by moving closer to the source of supply or by moving closer to the final customer by a continuation of the productive process. In the steel industry, for example, a steel fabricator may start with raw materials and produce the iron and steel, or he may move in the other direction and contract to erect steel structures for customers.

In extending operations back to the source of supply, a company is performing the services of its suppliers and is thereby extending the scope of its operations within the total industry. In doing so, the company hopes to realize the profits from this activity.

By extending the manufacturing process toward the customer, the company also has extended its scope of operations within the total industry and plans to earn the profits to be derived from more completed products.

THE MAKE OR BUY DECISION

A decision as to whether parts or components should be bought from suppliers or manufactured is a make or buy decision. Often additional facilities must be acquired if a company plans to produce its own parts, but in this chapter it is assumed that no additional investment is required and that the parts can be produced with the facilities that are available.

There are various factors that may influence a company in favor of producing its own parts or components. A few of the more important factors are listed here:

1. The company desires to operate as an integrated company.
2. There is freedom from dependence upon suppliers and their problems of production such as shortages of materials, strikes, etc.
3. Price increases announced by the suppliers will no longer be a problem.
4. Production schedules can be planned without reference to the delivery schedules of suppliers.
5. Profits can be earned by producing the parts.
6. By making its own parts, the company has better control over quality.

Any one of the advantages listed above may be the key to the decision, but it may not always be easy to measure the extent of the advantage in dollars. Insofar as possible, however, all factors entering into the decision should be stated in quantitative terms. The decision is based on a comparison of the costs to buy the parts with the costs to make the parts if other factors cannot be quantified and if weights are not assigned to these factors on a subjective basis.

In a make or buy decision, the point of indifference or break-even point is reached when the additional cost of making the parts is equal to the cost of buying the parts.

Additional cost to make the parts = Cost to buy the parts.

The decision is slanted in favor of making the parts if the cost to buy is greater than the additional cost to make.

Make the Parts

Additional cost to make the parts < Cost to buy the parts.

On the other hand, it is more economical to buy if the additional cost to make is greater than the cost to buy.

Buy the Parts

Additional cost to make the parts > Cost to buy the parts

The Incremental Costs

The additional or incremental cost of making the parts is the relevant cost in decision making. As explained in Chapter 8, the incremental cost is not only the variable cost attached to each unit to be produced, but is also the expected increase in fixed costs that will result from the decision.

In making any type of decision, all of the cost effects must be considered. Costs can be expected to increase if the company elects to make its own parts, but there may be some costs that can be reduced. For example, the cost to store the parts may be higher if they are purchased. By producing its own parts, a company may be able to synchronize its production schedules and hold the parts inventory to an absolute minimum, and in doing so reduce the costs of storage. The cost effect may also extend beyond the manufacturing area into the administrative area. An analysis to determine the cost effects should include all areas of operation so that *all* cost changes will be taken into account.

An Illustration of Make or Buy

At the present time, assume that a company is buying a part at a cost of $5.60 a unit and that the company can make this part with no additional investment. Approximately 100,000 units of this part are used each year. A special study has been made to determine how much it will cost to make this part, and the results of the study are given below.

Cost to make the part:

Direct materials	$ 245,000
Direct labor	121,000
Variable manufacturing overhead	43,000
Allocated portion of fixed manufacturing overhead	135,000
Increased fixed manufacturing overhead attributable to parts production	61,000
Increased administrative costs attributable to parts production	12,000
Total cost to make the part	$617,000
Total unit cost	
(617,000 ÷ 100,000 units)	$6.17

With all of the costs included, it appears that the part shouldn't be manufactured. There is certainly no advantage in making a part for $6.17 a unit when it can be purchased for $5.60.

The cost of $6.17 a unit as determined above may be the proper cost to enter in the accounting records *after* a decision has been made to produce the parts and while they are being manufactured. But it is not the correct cost for decision-making purposes. Costs that will be incurred whether the parts are made or not are sunk costs with respect to the decision and should be excluded in decisional analysis.

In this example, fixed manufacturing overhead of $135,000 has been allocated to parts production. But this overhead will be incurred whether the parts are made or not. Only the *changes* in costs are relevant. Assuming that all of the other costs listed are cost increases that can be expected from parts production, the analysis should be revised as follows:

Total cost to make the part	$617,000
Less the allocated fixed costs	135,000
Increased cost to make the part	$482,000
Increased unit cost (482,000 ÷ 100,000 units)	$ 4.82

It is now revealed that there is an economic advantage in making the parts, an advantage of $.78 per unit ($5.60 - $4.82) or a total cost advantage of $78,000.

The decisional analysis can be expressed in equation form as follows:

Cost to buy		Additional cost to
100,000 units	>	make 100,000 units
$560,000		$482,000

Or, if preferred, the comparison can be set up in the form of an income statement with the cost to buy taking the place of revenue. In a sense, the cost to buy is similar to revenue in that the additional cost to make is offset against the cost to buy to determine the profit advantage from making the parts.

Cost to buy	$560,000
Less additional cost to make	482,000
Advantage of parts production	$ 78,000

The Accounting Costs

After a decision has been made to produce the parts, costs are assigned to the manufactured parts in the conventional accounting manner. On a full costing (absorption costing) basis, the cost to manufacture each parts unit is $6.17. Does this mean that a mistake was made and that the parts should not have been produced after all? No, there has been no mistake. If all of the manufactured products are to bear a full share of the total manufacturing costs, then the parts should bear their share, too.

In this example it has been assumed that $135,000 of the fixed costs should be allocated to parts production. However, these costs are not increased or decreased by parts production.

What will happen to these costs if the parts are not manufactured? The costs will still be incurred and will either be assigned to some other production or charged off during the period as idle capacity costs. Therefore, these costs are not relevant in making a decision even though they may be apportioned over the various products in the accounting process of determining full product cost. These costs, it must be remembered, pertain to the *total* operation and not to any particular part of it.

Other Factors in the Decision

The decision to make parts cannot be based entirely upon direct economic analysis. The measureable economic advantage may favor parts production, but there may be other factors to be considered. The economic analysis then serves as a basing point in establishing values for the other factors that cannot easily be quantified.

Some of the factors that will tend to go against a decision to produce parts are listed below.

1. A supplier of parts may also be a customer. If he loses his status as a supplier, the company may lose a valuable customer.
2. Perhaps the company cannot produce the parts as efficiently as a supplier who specializes in this type of work.
3. Parts production may interfere to some extent with other productive activities.
4. The company may find it difficult to enter into competition with its suppliers.

One company, the author recalls, attempted to produce parts that it had been buying from outside suppliers, and in addition to producing parts for its own needs produced parts for sale on the general market. The former suppliers were small companies with relatively low overhead costs and were able to reduce their prices substantially. As a result, the company could not sell profitably to outsiders, and inasmuch as outside sales were an important factor in making a decision to produce the parts, the company would have been better off if it had continued to buy the parts. Hence, in making an evaluation, outside influences must be considered along with the internal cost effects.

COMPLETION OF AN INTERMEDIATE PRODUCT

As stated earlier, the manufacturing process can also be extended in the other direction, with additional work being done to finish a product that is presently being sold either as a partially completed product or as a component to be used in a final assembly. In this type of situation, the manufacturer is moving closer to the ultimate consumer of the end product, hoping, among other things, to earn the profits from this market. In addition, he may look for the advantages to be derived from selling to the final customers as compared with the problems of selling to other manufacturers.

In making a decision, the selling price of the final product less the additional cost to complete it is compared with the selling price of the intermediate product. An indifference or break-even point is reached when these two elements are brought into balance.

$$\begin{array}{ccc} \text{Selling price} & & \text{Selling price of final} \\ \text{of intermediate} & = & \text{product less additional} \\ \text{product} & & \text{cost to complete.} \end{array}$$

If the selling price of the intermediate product is greater than the difference between the selling price of the final product and the costs to complete it, then the decision is in favor of selling the intermediate product.

Selling price of intermediate product	>	Selling price of final product less additional cost to complete it.

Conversely, the decision is in favor of the final product if the revenue from its sale exceeds the additional costs of completion by more than the revenue to be derived from the intermediate product.

In making a decision of this type, consideration should be given to the effect of the decision on the rate of return. An alternative that may appear to be desirable may result in a reduced rate of return on the sales dollar and on the assets invested. Rate of return is a most important factor in the evaluation of management. Hence, the break-even type of analysis serves as a general guide in selecting a course of action. Further study should be made to determine the effect on the rate of return before making a final decision.

The Break-Even Point

The break-even equation may be expressed in another way if desired.

$$RF = CF + RI.$$

RF = revenue from final product
CF = additional cost to complete final product
RI = revenue from intermediate product

The revenue from the intermediate product is a cost of the finishing operation. It is an opportunity cost of the finishing operation. If the manufacturing process is continued, the company will have to sacrifice the revenue that could be obtained from the sale of the intermediate product. The sacrifice of this revenue has the same effect on the final profit as an additional cost.

The cost to make the intermediate product, however, is generally a sunk cost to be disregarded in decision making. The intermediate product will be manufactured in either case, and the cost to produce this product will be incurred whether the manufacturing process is extended or not.

A Decision to Continue the Productive Operation

Assume that a company can sell 150,000 units of an intermediate product for $6.00 a unit to obtain a total revenue of $900,000. By incurring additional costs of $300,000, it is possible to produce 100,000 units of a final product that can be sold for $14.00 a unit to obtain a revenue of $1,400,000. The sunk costs that are incurred to produce the intermediate product amount to $750,000.

In this example, there is an advantage in favor of continuing the manufacturing operation.

Revenue from sale of the completed product (100,000 units x $14.00)	$1,400,000
Cost to complete the product	$ 300,000
Opportunity cost revenue to be derived from the intermediate product (150,000 units x $6.00)	900,000
Total decisional costs	$1,200,000
Net advantage of continuing the manufacturing operation	$ 200,000

After a decision is made to extend the operation, profits may be measured on a full cost basis. The opportunity costs will no longer have significance, but the *total* cost to manufacture the product will be matched against revenue in profit determination. The income statement for this part of the operation is shown below.

Sales (100,000 units x $14.00)	$1,400,000
Cost to manufacture intermediate product	750,000
Additional cost to manufacture final product	300,000
*Allocated fixed cost to finishing operation	200,000
	$1,250,000
Net income	$ 150,000

*Assumed to be the amount of fixed overhead to be allocated to this operation on the basis of space and facilities used.

Under certain conditions, a portion of the cost to manufacture the intermediate product may not be a sunk cost but may have to be considered in deciding upon the extent of the manufacturing operation. Assume, for example, that some shrinkage can be expected in producing the final product, and that in order to get 100,000 units of the final product, 200,000 units of the intermediate product must be started in production. The market for the intermediate product, however, is limited to 150,000 units. If this is the case, the additional 50,000 units of intermediate product will be produced only to meet the final product requirements. Assume further that it will cost an additional $180,000 to manufacture 50,000 more units of the intermediate product. This particular cost is *not* a sunk cost but an additional cost that will be incurred to produce the final product. The revised analysis based on the new assumptions is set forth below.

Revenue from sale of the completed product (100,000 units x $14.00)	$1,400,000
Cost to complete the product	$ 300,000
Cost to produce additional units of the intermediate product for use in the final manufacturing operation	180,000
Opportunity cost, revenue to be derived from the intermediate product (150,000 units x $6.00)	900,000
Total decisional costs	$1,380,000
Net advantage of continuing the manufacturing operation	$ 20,000

In general it can be stated that a cost is *usually* a sunk cost or that is is *usually* not a sunk cost. This may be true in most cases, but there are exceptions as shown by a revision of the last example. Each case has to be examined separately to see if there are peculiarities that deserve special attention or if there are exceptions to the general rule. The analytical process to be followed in any situation is summarized below.

1. Determine the revenues and costs that will be affected by a decision and measure the extent of this effect.
2. Exclude all revenues and costs that will not be affected by the decision.

A TEMPORARY SHUTDOWN

Instead of being faced with the more pleasant prospect of improving profits by an extension of operations, a firm may be forced to curtail operations on a temporary basis in order to reduce losses. During a period of reduced demand for the product, it may be more economical to shut down the plant until increases in demand justify a resumption of operations. While the plant is closed, deliveries may be made to customers from inventories. The demand in excess of the amount that can be supplied from available inventories, however, may be too low to warrant continued production.

A Break-Even Point

The total costs of production may not be entirely recovered when the plant is operating too far below its normal capacity. Perhaps some of this loss can be avoided by closing the plant during a slack period. Certain costs, however, will continue whether the plant is open or closed. For example, to close the plant, it may be necessary to dismantle certain equipment or to protect it during a period of idleness. In addition, the costs to protect the plant against vandalism and theft may increase when the plant is closed. Then when the plant resumes operation, there will be added costs of getting the plant and equipment ready for production again.

There is a break-even point in deciding upon whether the plant should operate or close down. This point of economic indifference can be expressed in equation form as follows:

$$\text{Cost of shutdown} \quad = \quad \text{Loss from continued operation.}$$

There is a cost advantage in favor of shutdown if the cost of shutdown is less than the loss from continued operation.

$$\text{Cost of shutdown} \quad < \quad \text{Loss from continued operation.}$$

However, if the cost of shutdown is greater, the plant should remain open.

$$\text{Cost of shutdown} \quad > \quad \text{Loss from continued operation.}$$

A Shutdown Illustration

The shutdown decision is illustrated by assuming that a plant at normal capacity can produce 900,000 units of product at 450,000 machine hours. Each unit of product contributes $20 to fixed costs and profits. The fixed costs for a year amount to $6,000,000. Hence, the plant can earn a profit of $12,000,000 when it produces and sells at normal capacity [(900,000 units x $20) minus $6,000,000]. At 33-1/3 percent of normal capacity, the plant breaks even.

$$\text{Break-even point at 300,000 units of product} = \frac{\text{Fixed costs of } \$6,000,000}{\text{Unit contribution margin, } \$20}$$

$$\text{Break-even point as a percentage of normal capacity, 33-1/3\%} = \frac{\text{Break-even volume, 300,000 units}}{\text{Normal volume, 900,000 units}}$$

During the next year, however, the company anticipates a much lower demand for the product. In order to satisfy customer needs, the plant will operate at 90,000 machine hours and produce 180,000 units of product. The loss at this level of operation amounts to $2,400,000.

Fixed costs	$6,000,000
Less recovery of fixed costs from operations	
(180,000 units x $20 a unit contribution margin)	3,600,000
Loss (unrecovered fixed costs)	$2,400,000

This loss from continued operation is then compared with the costs that will be incurred if the plant is closed for a comparable period of time. Obviously, a valid comparison cannot be made if the shutdown costs are on one time basis while the fixed costs of operation are on another. All costs must be for the same time interval.

Some of the fixed costs can probably be reduced if the plant is closed. For example, certain indirect materials used for plant maintenance may not be needed if the plant is closed. Or, perhaps, some of the indirect labor, heat and light, repairs and maintenance, and various other costs can be reduced or eliminated during a period of shutdown. Assume for purposes of the illustration that the fixed costs can be reduced to $2,100,000 if the plant is closed.

However, there will be other costs that may increase with a plant shutdown. Costs to protect the plant and equipment, for example, are expected to increase by $140,000 during the shutdown period, and it is likely to cost an additional $30,000 to resume operations. The estimated costs associated with a shutdown are set forth below.

Fixed costs during shutdown period	$2,100,000
Additional costs during shutdown period	140,000
Startup costs at the conclusion of the the shutdown period	30,000
Total shutdown costs	$2,270,000

In the example given, plant losses can be reduced by closing the plant for a year.

Cost of shutdown $2,270,000   <   Loss from continued operation $2,400,000

Neither alternative is attractive, but it is better to lose $2,270,000 than to lose $2,400,000. As a practical matter, a year is a long shutdown period. Perhaps in this case a shutdown may be a prelude to a complete change in future plant utilization or to the sale of the plant. The shutdown decision may be only one in a chain of decisions that will have to be made.

It may be argued that the loss will be less than $2,270,000 because of sales from stockpiled inventories. True, the loss in total can be reduced by sales from inventories. However, these sales will be made whether the plant is open or closed and have no bearing on the decision itself.

A shutdown point or break-even point in making a shutdown decision is reached when the contribution from continued operation is equal to the difference between the fixed costs while operating and the shutdown costs.

$$\begin{array}{l} \text{Shutdown point} \\ \text{(a break-even point)} \end{array} = \frac{\begin{array}{c}\text{Fixed costs} \quad \text{Shutdown} \\ \text{of operation} - \text{costs}\end{array}}{\text{Unit contribution margin}}$$

$$\text{Shutdown point} = \frac{\$6,000,000 - \$2,270,000}{\$20}$$

$$\text{Shutdown point} = 186,500 \text{ units.}$$

If demand can be satisifed by producing only 186,500 units, the company will be indifferent as to whether the plant is open or not. The losses will be the same in either case.

Loss by operating:	
Fixed costs	$6,000,000
Less recovery of fixed costs from operations	
(186,500 units x $20 unit contribution margin)	3,730,000
Loss (unrecovered fixed costs)	$2,270,000
Loss by shutdown:	
Shutdown costs	$2,270,000

The shutdown point expressed as a percentage of normal capacity is between 20 and 21 percent,

$$\frac{186,500 \text{ units}}{900,000 \text{ units}} = 20.7\%$$

Other Factors in the Decision

Economic analysis may indicate that the plant should be closed, but, as in many other decisional situations, there will be factors that may influence a decision in the opposite direction. There are several disadvantages of plant shutdown that must be considered before making a decision.

1. The possibility of vandalism and theft.
2. Deterioration of idle facilities.
3. A loss of customers.
4. A loss of employees.
5. Effects on employee morale.
6. The difficulty of resuming operations.

Perhaps a certain amount of loss from operations may be accepted even though it would appear to be more economical to close the plant. In the example given, the advantage in favor of shutdown amounts to $130,000. If the company decides to continue operations in spite of the cost disadvantage, it has apparently placed a value of at least $130,000 on one or more of the disadvantages associated with shutdown.

SUMMARY

Operations may be extended either by producing the parts that are used to make the present product line or by doing further work on the present line to create a more finished product. Or operations may be contracted by purchasing a part that is now being manufactured or by discontinuing a finishing operation on a certain product line. A decision to expand or contract depends upon the increases or decreases in revenues and costs that can be expected from each alternative, with all other factors being recognized before making a selection.

A shutdown decision is a decision to close down operations for a limited period of time—a special type of contraction. The shutdown point is reached when the costs of shutdown are equal to the unrecovered fixed costs of continued operation. In some cases a measured economic advantage from shutdown may be sacrificed if management places more weight on certain disadvantages that cannot be measured precisely.

11

Planning the Flow
of Net Working Capital

An adequate investment in current resources must be maintained to support a successful business operation. If goods and services are to be rendered to customers, it may be necessary to have a certain amount invested in materials and parts used in production and in an inventory of finished products ready for delivery to customers. Also, cash must be held to pay the various costs of operation, and a certain amount of "cash in process" will most likely be held in the form of accounts receivable and temporary investments.

In this chapter no attempt will be made to determine how much should be invested in current resources to support operations. The amount to be invested will vary according to the requirements of the industry and the peculiar circumstances of the company, and no general rule can be given. Attention, however, will be directed to the problem of how current resources can be obtained from operating activity.

The important current resources, or, in other words, the current assets are listed below.

> Cash
> Temporary investments
> Accounts receivable
> Inventories
> Prepaid expenses

The prepaid expenses are included as current assets. If the operating expenses had not been paid in advance, the cash balance would be higher.

There are also current claims against a business entity for various services and materials received. Typical current claims or current liabilities are listed on the following page.

Accounts payable
Accrued wages and payroll taxes
Federal and state income taxes payable
Other accrued operating expenses

The excess of the current assets over the current liabilities is designated as *net working capital.* Current assets and current liabilities are constantly changing during the course of business operations. As sales are made, for example, inventories are reduced and the amounts to be collected from the customers are recorded. Various business obligations for rent, wages, insurance, taxes, and other operating items are recognized as liabilities and are paid at the proper times.

SOURCES AND USES OF NET WORKING CAPITAL

Without question, net working capital is a vital factor in business operation, hence it is quite important to find out where net working capital comes from and where it goes. As would be expected, the customers are an important source of net working capital. As sales are made, net working capital is increased by increasing the accounts receivable or cash. At the same time, net working capital is reduced by delivering inventories to the customers and by incurring various operating expenses. The net increase in net working capital that results from rendering goods and services to customers is the net increase in net working capital from operations.

In addition to operations, there are other sources of net working capital. For example, additional capital stock may be issued to stockholders in exchange for current assets. Typical sources of net working capital are listed here.

1. Operations.
2. Investment by stockholders.
3. Long-term borrowing.
4. The sale of plant assets or
   other non-current assets.

Net working capital is also used in various ways as indicated below.
1. Acquisition of non-current assets such as plant and equipment, patents,
   or stock in another company.
2. Payment of long-term debt.
3. Acquisition of the company's outstanding capital stock.
4. Payment of dividends.

Net working capital flows must be estimated in planning future operations. As stated before, a certain amount of net working capital must be held at all times to support a given level of operations. In addition, if an expansion is contemplated, the company will need even more net working capital to support the enlarged operation, to pay off long-term debt incurred as a result of the expansion, and to pay dividends to the stockholders. In drawing up plans for the future, management must estimate the inflows and outflows that can be expected from anticipated projects or other commitments.

NET WORKING CAPITAL AND NET INCOME

Operations are an important source of net working capital, and a careful distinction must be made between net working capital derived from operations and net income. Unfortunately, the net inflow of net working capital from operations is often considered to be virtually the same as net income. However, there is a very distinct difference, and this difference must be recognized.

Net income is the difference between revenues and expenses and is the measurement of the net inflow or outflow of net assets that results from rendering goods and services to customers. No particular type of asset is specified. Increases and decreases in *all* types of assets are included. The only stipulation is that the net assets increase or decrease as a result of the earning process. Ordinarily, current assets are received when sales are made to customers, but this may not always be true. Machinery or equipment may be received in exchange for goods or services. In this case, net income or loss would be measured as the difference between the value of the machinery or equipment received and the cost of the goods or services given in exchange. However, this transaction would not increase net working capital.

The net inflow of net working capital from operations is literally the net inflow of net working capital from operations—current assets reduced by current liabilities. Only the revenues and expenses that measure inflows and outflows of net working capital are included in the measurement of the flow of net working capital from operations. For example, depreciation is deducted as an expense on an income statement as a measurement of the amount of the cost of a plant asset that is to be offset against revenue in the determination of net income. The plant assets, however, are not a part of net working capital. Therefore, depreciation expense is not deducted in computing the net inflow of net working capital from operations.

A FLOW OF NET WORKING CAPITAL FROM OPERATIONS

Often an income statement is used as a starting point in computing the net inflow of net working capital from operations. The final net income is adjusted to a net working capital flow by adding back deductions that do not reduce net working capital and by subtracting additions that do not increase net working capital. In many cases depreciation, amortization of patents, gains or losses on the sale of plant assets or long-term investments, and amortization of premiums or discounts on debt issues are items that must be removed from an income statement to obtain the net working capital effect from operations.

An example showing how net income can be converted to a net working capital flow is given below.

Sales	$500,000
Cost of goods sold	$240,000
Wages and salaries	56,500
Heat and light	3,800
Depreciation	47,000
Insurance and taxes	11,600

Amortization of patents	8,300
Total operating expenses	$367,200
Net operating income	$132,800
Gain on sale of machinery	14,000
Net income before income taxes	$146,800
Federal and state income taxes	74,100
Net income after income taxes	$ 72,700

The items shown in italics do not affect the net working capital flow from operations and should be eliminated. Depreciation and amortization of patents reduce plant assets and patents respectively, but there is no reduction of current assets or increase in current liabilities. The sale of machinery will increase net working capital, but machinery is not sold in the normal course of operations. The proceeds from the sale of machinery, both the gain and the recovery of cost, are reported separately as a source of net working capital. The gain on the sale cannot be included as a source of net working capital from operations.

A computation of the net inflow of net working capital from operations is given below.

Net income after income taxes	$72,700
Add: Depreciation	47,000
Amortization of patents	8,300
	$128,000
Deduct gain on the sale of machinery	14,000
Net inflow of net working capital from operations	$114,000

In some cases there may be a net inflow of net working capital from operations even when there is a net loss reported on the income statement. This will be true if revenue exceeds the costs that require the expenditure of net working capital but not the total costs of operation. For example, assume that a net loss of $35,000 is shown on the income statement after deducting depreciation of $62,000. The net working capital received from operations amounts to $27,000.

Net loss	($35,000)
Add depreciation	62,000
Net inflow of net working capital from operations	$27,000

A FUNDS FLOW STATEMENT

Often net working capital is defined in a general way as funds, and a statement of the sources and uses of net working capital may also be designated as a statement of the sources and uses of funds. Customarily a statement of the sources and uses of funds is presented as shown below with the total uses of funds subtracted from the total sources to arrive at a net inflow or a net outflow.

Sources of funds:

Operations:

Net income	$ 482,000	
Add depreciation	78,000	$ 560,000
Proceeds from the sale of plant assets		54,000
Total sources of funds		$ 614,000

Uses of funds:

Expansion of plant	$ 330,000
Retirement of long-term debt	40,000
Payment of dividends	150,000
Total uses of funds	$ 520,000
Net inflow of funds	$ 94,000

In planning operations, estimates of the inflows and outflows may be rearranged to call attention to the important relationship between the funds supplied by operations and the desired uses. An estimated statement of the sources and uses of funds may be prepared as shown below.

Estimated funds to be provided by operating activity	$720,000
Less requirement for debt retirement	140,000
Balance remaining after debt retirement	$580,000
Less dividends to stockholders	170,000
Balance after debt retirement and dividends	$410,000
Approved capital expenditures	280,000
Balance (or deficiency) after approved capital expenditures	$130,000
Add anticipated proceeds from the sale of plant assets and long-term investments	46,000
Balance remaining (or deficiency to be financed)	$176,000

PLANNING THE FUNDS FLOW REQUIREMENTS

Inasmuch as net working capital is so important in supporting operations and future growth, plans must be made to obtain sufficient net working capital and to apply it as needed for carefully selected purposes. Net working capital can be obtained by selling plant assets and long-term investments and by issuing capital stock or long-term debt; but, in the long run, operations are expected to be a major source of net working capital.

The estimated net working capital requirements and the estimated net inflow from operations can be brought together in a break-even type of equation.

Net working capital from operations   =   Net working capital required.

The need for net working capital during the year can be estimated with plans drawn up to show how much must be provided from operations to meet this objective. If it is unrealistic to expect operations to meet the entire requirement, plans may be made to obtain the difference in another way or to scale down the requirements.

A BREAK-EVEN SOLUTION

The conventional break-even equation to solve for the sales revenue at the point of no profit or loss is given below.

$$\text{Sales revenue at break-even point of no profit or loss} = \frac{\text{Fixed costs}}{\text{Contribution margin percentage}}$$

This equation can be modified to solve for the sales revenue that will cover only the costs that require the use of net working capital. At this point there is neither an inflow nor an outflow of net working capital from operations. In other words, it is a break-even point for the net working capital flow from operations.

As already stated, there may be expenses on an income statement that do not decrease net working capital. Depreciation is an expense of this sort and will be used here as an example. The break-even point for a net working flow from operations can be computed by subtracting expenses that do not reduce net working capital from the fixed costs.

$$\text{Sales revenue at break-even point, net working capital flow} = \frac{\text{Fixed costs} - \text{Depreciation and expenses not reducing net working capital}}{\text{Contribution margin percentage}}$$

Assume that a company has annual fixed costs of $600,000 and that included in these costs is depreciation of $90,000. The contribution margin is equal to 30 percent of sales revenue.

$$\text{Sales revenue at break-even point, net working capital flow} = \frac{\$600,000 - \$90,000}{.30}$$

$$\text{Sales revenue at break-even point, net working capital flow} = \$1,700,000.$$

With a sales revenue of $1,700,000, the company will not increase or decrease its net working capital as a result of its operating activity.

Sales	$1,700,000
Variable costs (70% of sales)	1,190,000
Contribution margin	$ 510,000
Fixed costs	600,000
Loss on operation	($ 90,000)
Add depreciation	90,000
Break-even point, net working capital flow	-0-

At this point, note that the company does not break even on a profit or loss basis. The depreciation expense is not covered. In order to break even on a profit or loss basis, sales revenue must be $2,000,000.

$$\text{Sales revenue to break even on a profit or loss basis} = \frac{\$600,000}{.30}$$

$$\text{Sales revenue to break even} = \$2,000,000.$$

THE INCOME TAX EFFECT

When income taxes are considered, an additional computation must be made. If an expense that does not require the expenditure of net working capital is deductible in computing income taxes, the expense has an *indirect effect on net working capital* by reducing income taxes and thereby conserving net working capital that would otherwise be paid out in taxes. Conversely, a credit on the income statement that does not bring in net working capital may increase income taxes and thus reduce net working capital.

A Tax Saving

In the example just given, assume that there is a 40 percent income tax rate. With a $90,000 loss on operations (equal to the depreciation), the company receives a tax benefit of $36,000. The tax saving from the depreciation deduction in this case can be applied against income taxes paid in earlier years, or it can be carried forward and offset against taxes in future years. The important point is that the depreciation deduction helped to conserve net working capital by reducing income taxes. When income taxes are considered, the company does not break even on a net working capital basis with sales of $1,700,000. Actually, there is an increase of net working capital from operations of $36,000—the tax saving from the depreciation deduction.

To obtain the true break-even point on a net working capital basis, revenue must be reduced even further to eliminate the tax saving of $36,000. The equations to be developed on the following pages can be simplified by using the symbols defined below.

SR   = sales revenue at break-even point of no increase or decrease in net working capital from operations.

CMP = contribution margin percentage.

FC   = fixed costs.

D   = depreciation or other expenses not requiring the use of net working capital.

CTR = complement of the income tax rate (100% minus the tax rate).

TS   = tax saving from an expense that does not require the use of net working capital.

TI   = tax increase from a revenue or credit that does not increase net working capital.

DWC = desired net inflow of net working capital from operations.

152   PLANNING THE FLOW OF NET WORKING CAPITAL

The first step in compensating for the tax saving is to recognize that the tax saving can be offset by an equivalent reduction in the contribution margin *after* income taxes.

Tax saving = Reduction of contribution margin *after* income taxes.

Next, the reduction of the contribution margin *after* taxes must be converted to a reduction of the contribution margin *before* taxes. Remember that the contribution margin itself is subject to income taxes. To solve for the reduction of the contribution margin *before* taxes, divide the reduction of the contribution margin *after* taxes by the complement of the income tax rate.

$$\text{Reduction in contribution margin } before \text{ taxes} = \frac{\text{Reduction in contribution margin } after \text{ taxes}}{\text{Complement of income tax rate}}$$

Inasmuch as the tax saving is to be equal to the reduction in contribution margin *after* taxes, the tax saving can be substituted in the equation as shown below.

$$\text{Reduction in contribution margin } before \text{ taxes} = \frac{TS}{CTR}$$

$$\text{Reduction in contribution margin } before \text{ taxes} = \frac{\$36,000}{.6}$$

$$\text{Reduction in contribution margin } before \text{ taxes} = \$60,000.$$

A reduction in the contribution margin before taxes of $60,000 will compensate for a tax saving of $36,000 from the depreciation deduction.

Reduction in contribution margin *before* taxes (100%)	$60,000
Income taxes on the reduction in the contribution margin (40% tax rate)	24,000
Reduction in contribution margin *after* taxes (60% complement of tax rate)	$36,000

A reduction in the contribution margin after taxes of $36,000 is equal to the tax saving from depreciation.

The small equation given for computing the reduction of the contribution margin before taxes is handled like a desired profit in the conventional break-even equation. Instead of being added, however, it is subtracted. Remember that the objective is to find the amount of the *reduction* that will balance out a tax saving.

$$SR = \frac{FC - D - \frac{TS}{CTR}}{CMP}$$

$$SR = \frac{\$600,000 - \$90,000 - \frac{\$36,000}{.6}}{.3}$$

$$SR = \$1,500,000.$$

A proof is given below.

Sales	$1,500,000
Variable costs (70% of sales)	1,050,000
Contribution margin	$ 450,000
Fixed costs	600,000
Net loss before taxes	($ 150,000)
Tax reduction arising from loss (40% of loss)	60,000
Net loss after tax	($ 90,000)
Add depreciation	90,000
Break-even point, net working capital flow	- 0 -

A Tax Increase

An income statement may also include revenue or credits that do not increase the net working capital from operations. For example, a gain may be reported from the sale of an investment in stock or from the sale of a piece of equipment. The credit or gain, if subject to income tax, will *increase* income taxes. If operations are expected to absorb this increase in taxes, then the increase must be included in the break-even equation. The tax increase is handled like the tax saving with the exception that the contribution margin must be increased to compensate for the additional tax.

Continuing with the example given, assume that a gain of $288,000 is expected from the sale of a long-term investment. The gain is taxed at a rate of 25 percent and will increase income taxes by $72,000. The rate of tax on the gain is not used in the break-even computation. The amount of the increase in the tax, however, is significant. In making the break-even computations, the ordinary income tax rate is used. Remember that the objective is to determine the additional contribution margin that will be needed to offset the amount of the tax on the gain, and the contribution margin will be taxed at ordinary income tax rates.

A complete break-even equation is now given for a net working capital flow from operations based on the assumption that operations are expected to absorb the tax on the gain.

$$SR = \frac{FC - D - \dfrac{TS}{CTR} + \dfrac{TI}{CTR}}{CMP}$$

$$SR = \frac{\$600,000 - \$90,000 - \dfrac{\$36,000}{.6} + \dfrac{\$72,000}{.6}}{.3}$$

$$SR = \$1,900,000$$

A proof of the solution follows.

Sales	$1,900,000
Variable costs (70% of sales)	1,330,000
Contributing margin	$ 570,000
Fixed costs	600,000
Net operating loss	($ 30,000)
Gain on sale of long-term investment	288,000
Net income before income taxes	$ 258,000
Income taxes (25% of $288,000 minus 40% of $30,000)	60,000
Net income after income taxes	$ 198,000
Add depreciation	90,000
	$ 288,000
Less gain on sale of long-term investment	288,000
Break-even point, net working capital flow	—0—

A Desired Inflow from Operations

The conventional profit and loss break-even equation can be adapted for use in computing a desired profit. Similarly, the break-even equation for the net working capital flow can be expanded to include a planned or desired net inflow from operations. The desired inflow of net working capital or funds, designated in the equation as DFF, is handled like the desired profit from operations in a conventional profit and loss break-even equation.

Returning to the previous example, assume that operations are expected to increase net working capital by $360,000. The sales revenue required to meet this objective is computed below.

$$SR = \frac{FC - D - \dfrac{TS}{CTR} + \dfrac{TI}{CTR} + \dfrac{DFF}{CTR}}{CMP}$$

$$SR = \frac{\$600,000 - \$90,000 - \dfrac{\$36,000}{.6} + \dfrac{\$72,000}{.6} + \dfrac{\$360,000}{.6}}{.3}$$

$$SR = \$3,900,000$$

With sales of $3,900,000, the net working capital will increase by $360,000 as shown below.

Sales	$3,900,000
Variable costs (70% of sales)	2,730,000
Contribution margin	$1,170,000
Fixed costs	600,000
Net operating income	$ 570,000
Gain on sale of long-term investment	288,000
Net income before income taxes	$ 858,000
Income taxes (25% of $288,000 plus 40% of $570,000)	300,000
Net income after income taxes	$ 558,000
Add depreciation	90,000
	$ 648,000
Less gain on sale of long-term investment	288,000
Desired net working capital flow from operations	$ 360,000

ADVANTAGES OF THE BREAK-EVEN EQUATION

Seemingly the equation that has been developed in this chapter is a complicated approach to a fairly simple problem. The same result can be obtained by starting with the desired net working capital flow from operations and working back through a statement form to the net sales. If this is so, why bother with the equation? Admittedly, the problem can be solved without an equation, but the equation does have some distinct advantages.

1. The equation is no more difficult than any other form of solution if the terms are understood.
2. In the equation everything is brought together in a concise form.
3. The equation provides a useful algorithm for problem solving by computer.
4. By setting up factors in an equation, it is easier to see how each factor influences the final result.

Values can be assigned to variables by a computer program in several different combinations to find out what will happen if one or more of the variables changes. The effect of the changes can be determined quite easily by a computer operation.

In simple cases, the effect of any particular change can be derived from a manual computation. For example, assume that depreciation is to be reduced by $18,000. The income tax rate is 40 percent, and there is a 30 percent contribution margin. With a reduction of $18,000 in depreciation, there will be an increase in income taxes of $7,200 (40% of $18,000). How much additional sales revenue will be required to compensate for the tax effect? A tax increase of $7,200 has the same effect on net working capital as a contribution margin before taxes of $12,000 ($7,200 ÷ .6). And a contribution margin before taxes of $12,000 can be derived from a sales revenue of $40,000 ($12,000 ÷ .3).

$$\frac{TS}{CTR} \bigg/ CMP = \frac{\$7200}{6} \bigg/ .3 = \$40,000.$$

Hence, an increase of $40,000 in sales will make up for an increase of $7,200 in taxes that results from reduced depreciation. The net working capital flow from operations will be unchanged when the increased flow from additional sales is balanced against the tax increase.

Increased tax resulting from decreased depreciation		$7,200
Less net working capital increase from increased sales:		
Sales revenue	$40,000	
Variable costs (70%)	28,000	
Contribution margin	$12,000	
Tax on contribution margin (40%)	4,800	
Increase in net working capital		7,200
Net working capital balancing point or break-even point		- 0 -

As demonstrated above, the equation can be applied to determine what must be done to compensate for the effect of some anticipated change. There are many possibilities. For instance, the last example could have been examined from another point of view. Sales revenue is expected to decrease by $40,000. How much more depreciation should be deducted to balance the effect on net working capital? In this case, one more step must be added in order to solve for the depreciation. The tax saving from depreciation may be expressed as D x .4.

$$\frac{D \times .4}{.6} \bigg/ .3 = \$40,000$$

$$D \times .4 = .6 \times .3 \times \$40,000$$

$$D = \frac{.6 \times .3 \times \$40,000}{.4}$$

$$D = \frac{\$7,200}{.4}$$

$$D = \$18,000$$

SUMMARY

In conducting business, a certain amount of net working capital must be available to provide for payments to creditors for various materials and services obtained. And an inventory should be on hand to serve the needs of production and to meet delivery schedules. If expansion is contemplated, additional net working capital must be provided to cover the costs of expansion and to support the expanded operation.

Operational activity is expected to produce additional net working capital, and a break-even type of equation can be used to solve the sales revenue that will produce the required net working capital. The equation is easy to use and can be adapted to a computer operation. The equation can help to determine the effect of certain changes on the net working capital flow, or it may be used to search for ways to balance out the effect of some anticipated change.

12

Selecting the Best
Capital Investment Alternative

An investment is made with the expectation that a benefit will be derived to justify the sacrifice—the amount invested. A merchant will invest money in goods that he expects to sell to customers, or a manufacturer will invest in materials and services to create a product that he can sell. Often relatively little time will elapse between the time that the investment is made and the time that the benefits are received.

A capital investment, however, differs from a short-run type of investment in that the investment and the related benefits are not on the same time basis. A capital investment, for example, may be made at the present time with benefits expected over a period of years extending into the future. Typically, the investment may be a new building; machinery or equipment; a structure; or an investment in stocks, bonds, or real estate. But a capital investment is not necessarily an investment in tangible property. It may take the form of an investment in services for the development of a new product line or for the promotion of sales. The point is that the investment, whatever form it takes, is separated from the benefits or returns by a lapse of time.

Often an investment will be made in its entirety in the present, but this will not always be true. Part of the investment may be made in the future. For example, a large piece of equipment may be purchased now, but it is anticipated that major part replacements will have to be made at various future dates. The total investment in the equipment then, like the returns, will be spread over future time periods.

The returns are usually thought of as being positive inflows in the form of dividends, interest, rentals, or profits depending upon the nature of the investment. Some investments, however, are not expected to yield inflows. Instead, they will produce cost savings; inasmuch as cost savings increase profits, these investments yield benefits by reducing outflows. A machine, for example, may be replaced with a more efficient machine that will reduce materials, labor, and overhead costs. No additional revenue is anticipated, but the benefit is derived from the saving in costs.

157

A capital investment decision is a difficult type of decision to make because of the time element. The future, of course, is uncertain, yet both the investment and the benefits that pertain to future years must be estimated as accurately as possible. In addition, a comparison of the investment and the returns or benefits cannot be made unless all monetary amounts are stated on the same time basis. Hence, future amounts must be discounted to a present value using an appropriate discount rate.

Three basic elements are brought together in the capital investment decision:

1. The investment.
2. The expected returns.
3. The minimum rate of return.

The capital investment decision, as will be discussed in this chapter, is the decision to select one alternative out of many that may be available for a given investment situation. The total capital expenditure program will not be considered. Instead, it will be assumed that the company is interested in a given project or situation. Is there any candidate that will meet the rate-of-return objective and if there are competing candidates, which candidate is best? This is the type of problem that will be discussed—the selection of the best alternative for the investment situation.

THE INVESTMENT

The net amount invested for decision-making purposes is not necessarily the amount to be entered in the accounting records if the investment is made. For decision-making purposes, the investment is either the net outflow of net working capital or the sacrifice of a net inflow of net working capital that will result from the decision to invest. The expected outlay for the investment itself may be only part of the total investment. Other related factors may enter the picture and have to be considered in computing the total or net amount invested.

To illustrate, it is assumed that a certain machine can be purchased, delivered, and installed at the following cost:

Invoice cost of machine	$38,000
Freight and delivery cost	700
Installation cost	1,100
Total accounting cost	$39,800

If the machine is acquired, the accounting cost of $39,800 will be entered in the records and accounted for as the cost of the machine itself. However, if the new machine is bought, the company plans to sell an old machine for $12,000. The purchase of the new machine and the sale of the old machine are linked together as two parts of *one* decision. The undepreciated cost of the old machine is $8,000; if it is sold for $12,000, there will be a gain of $4,000 on the sale. It is estimated that there will be a $1,000 income tax on the gain. Therefore, the *net* benefit to be derived from selling the old machine is $11,000—the gross proceeds of $12,000 received from the sale minus the $1,000 tax on the gain.

The net amount invested in the new machine is the cost of the new machine minus the net amount that can be received from the sale of the old machine.

Outlay for new machine		$39,800
Less:		
Proceeds from sale of old machine	$12,000	
Less tax on $4,000 gain	1,000	
Net proceeds from sale of old machine		11,000
Net investment (decision-making purposes)		$28,800

If a loss is to be expected on the sale of the old machine, the tax saving from the loss will be added to the proceeds from such sale. The total benefit from the sale is equal to the gross amount received from the sale plus the reduction in taxes arising from the loss deduction. The total benefit to be derived from selling the old machine is subtracted from the cost of the new machine in computing the net investment for the decision. Suppose, for example, that the old machine can be sold for $4,000 instead of $12,000 and that the tax benefit from the loss deduction amounts to $1,000. The net investment would then be computed as follows:

Outlay for new machine		$39,800
Less:		
Proceeds from sale of old machine	$4,000	
Add tax saving from $4,000 loss deduction	1,000	
Net proceeds from sale of old machine		5,000
Net investment (decision-making purposes)		$34,800

Sometimes an investment is a project such as a new plant for the production of a new product line. To support the new product line, additional net working capital will be required. The additional net working capital that must be held to support the investment is as much a part of the total investment as the cost of the plant and equipment itself. Resources that must be held in the form of cash, accounts receivable, and inventory are committed to the project just as much as the resources that are committed to buildings, structures, machinery, and equipment. The cost of the plant and the equipment, for example, may be estimated at $3,850,000, and the net working capital required to sustain the project may be estimated at $750,000. The net investment for decision-making purposes is then $4,600,000, as shown below.

Net investment in plant and equipment	$3,850,000
Estimated net working capital requirement (distributed over cash, accounts receivable, and inventory as reduced by normal increase in current liabilities to finance the requirement)	750,000
Net investment in project	$4,600,000

There may be other factors to be considered in the investment decision. For example, if a new piece of equipment is acquired, the company may save the cost of overhauling an old machine that would otherwise be rehabilitated and continued in service. The saving in the costs of overhauling the old equipment minus the tax benefit to be derived from deducting the costs for income taxes should be deducted in computing the net investment.

A new piece of equipment, for example, may cost $25,000. If this equipment is purchased, the company will not incur costs of $6,000 to rehabilitate old equipment. The rehabilitation costs can be avoided if the new equipment is obtained. However, the costs of rehabilitation may be deducted in computing income taxes, and if deducted will reduce income taxes by $3,000. Therefore, the net cost of rehabilitation after income taxes amounts to $3,000. The net investment for the decision is computed below.

Cost of new equipment		$25,000
Less:		
Avoided costs of rehabilitation on old equipment	$6,000	
Less income tax benefit of cost deduction	3,000	
Net benefit from avoided costs		3,000
Net investment (decision-making purposes)		$22,000

If avoided costs are to be deducted in arriving at the net amount to be invested, they must be carefully considered. Sometimes it may appear that a cost will be avoided, but in practice the cost will still be incurred. Wishful thinking about potential cost reductions should not be introduced in an effort to rationalize in favor of investment. In the example given, the company may decide to rehabilitate the old equipment in any case. Hence, the cost will not be avoided and should not be included in the analysis. The inclusion or exclusion of the avoided costs depends upon the actual intentions of management.

The important point to remember in all investment situations is that *all* effects on net working capital that are related to the investment must be taken into account. Sometimes these effects will be in the form of additional investment in auxiliary tools, additional working capital to support the investment, a saving in rehabilitation costs after taxes, or a reduction in net investment arising from the sale of other assets related to the investment situation.

THE EXPECTED RETURNS

The returns from an investment are the benefits to be derived from the investment over the years and are generally measured either as the net inflows of net working capital or the savings in net outflows of net working capital. Sometimes the net working capital flows are loosely referred to as cash flows. In making long-range estimates, however, it is difficult to predict the literal flow of cash. Hence, net working capital flow (current assets minus current liabilities) is estimated as a broad approximation of the long-range cash flow effect.

Assume that a new project is expected to produce additional revenues of $800,000 each year and that the additional variable and fixed costs (excluding depreciation but including income taxes) are estimated at $300,000 each year. The annual return is then $500,000, as computed below.

Incremental revenues	$800.000
Incremental costs (excluding depreciation but including income taxes)	300,000
Net return (net inflow of net working capital)	$500,000

Depreciation on the investment is not included as a cost in computing the returns. The net working capital return, not the profit, is to be related to the investment.

As stated before, some investments are not expected to yield additional net working capital. Instead, they are expected to reduce the outflow of net working capital. In the example given below, the equipment yields net cost advantages but does not produce additional revenue.

Anticipated annual cost savings:	
Reduced materials cost	$16,000
Reduced labor cost	15,000
Reduced fuel and lubrication cost	4,000
Total cost reductions	$35,000
Anticipated annual cost increases:	
Increased repairs and maintenance cost	$ 3,500
Increased insurance cost	1,200
Total cost increases	$ 4,700
Net cost saving before incoome taxes	$30,300
Less increased income taxes on net cost savings (including effect of depreciation on income taxes)	15,600
Net cost saving after income taxes	$14,700

The net cost saving after income taxes is the net working capital return expected from this investment alternative.

The Depreciation Effect

As pointed out in the preceding chapter, depreciation does not require an expenditure of net working capital. However, depreciation is deducted for income taxes, and as a result income taxes are lower than they would be otherwise. Therefore, depreciation has an indirect effect on net working capital by reducing income taxes.

Assume, for example, that an investment is expected to produce an annual cost saving before income taxes of $40,500. Depreciation on the investment is estimated at $15,000 each year, and there is a 40 percent income tax rate. The income tax on the cost saving of $40,500 amounts to $16,200 (40 percent of $40,500). The depreciation deduction of $15,000, however, will reduce income taxes by $6,000. Thus, the net income tax is $10,200, and the net cost saving after income taxes is $30,300, as shown below.

Net cost saving before income taxes		$40,500
Less income taxes:		
Increased tax from reduced costs	$16,200	
Less tax saving from depreciation	6,000	
Net income tax		10,200
Net cost saving after income taxes		$30,300

Residual Returns

In addition to the regular returns expected over the years, there may be residual returns at the termination of the investment. At the end of the life of the investment, a building, machine, or other type of asset may be sold, and the proceeds from the sale is a return of the final year. Likewise, net working capital that has been held to support a project will no longer be needed when a project is terminated and may be released for other purposes. The released net working capital is also a return of the final year.

THE MINIMUM RATE OF RETURN

In making an investment decision, the net investment and the returns over the years are brought together. As stated earlier, the investment and the returns are not on the same time basis. Present dollar amounts can only be compared with future dollar amounts when the time element is recognized through the use of an interest rate or a discount rate. Customarily the problem is handled by discounting future dollar amounts to a present value. However, if a valid comparison is to be made, the discount rate to be used in making the conversion must be selected carefully.

The discount rate is not the rate to be paid on borrowed money nor is it necessarily the rate of return that has been earned in the past from similar investment situations. Instead, the minimum acceptable rate of return is the lowest rate of return that can be expected in *future years* from an investment situation.

The threshold rate of return, that is, the lowest rate that the company is willing to accept, is the rate that it can expected to receive in the future. The minimum rate of return is then an opportunity cost rate of return. If other investments can yield this rate, there is no point in decreasing the overall rate of return by selecting a less productive investment. To be acceptable, even on a marginal basis, an investment must yield returns that when discounted at this minimum rate are at least equal to the present value of the investment.

THE POINT OF DECISION

The break-even point or point of decision is reached when the present value of the returns expected from the investment candidate is equal to the present value of the. investment.

Present value of returns = Present value of investment.

When both the investment and the related returns are discounted to a present value at the lowest acceptable rate of return, there is neither advantage or disadvantage from the investment if the amounts are equal.

Advantage lies in favor of the investment, however, if the present value of the returns is greater than the present value of the investment.

Present value of returns > Present value of investment.

Conversely, there is a disadvantage if the present value of the returns is less than the present value of the investment.

Present value of returns < Present value of investment.

AN INVESTMENT DECISION

In making an investment decision, the objective is to select the best candidate for a given investment situation. Several candidates or alternatives may be available, but only one is to be chosen. The best alternative is not only the best one for the situation but is also the one that is expected to yield the greatest economic advantage.

Sometimes an economic advantage will be difficult to measure. Not all investments are made with the expectation of receiving direct measureable returns. A company will sometimes be interested in investments that are expected to enhance the public image of the company and to help society in general. This type of investment also yields a return in a sense, but the return can only be measured in a general way. In this chapter, however, it is assumed that the expected returns can be set forth in monetary terms. Values that cannot be easily measured by quantitative means will be discussed in the last chapter.

To be acceptable on a marginal basis, a candidate for investment must produce returns that on a present value basis are equal to the present value of the investment. The best candidate, however, is the one that can produce the largest excess of returns over the investment—with both the returns and the investment stated on a present value basis.

For a particular investment situation, assume that two alternatives are available. In both cases, the total investment is to be made at the present time and returns are expected over each of the next five years.

Investment Alternatives

	A	B
Net investment	$35,000	$70,000
Estimated annual return for each of 5 years	14,000	25,000

The lowest acceptable rate of return is 15 percent. This means that investments can be expected to earn 15 percent in the future and that returns received in future years can be reinvested to yield 15 percent. An investment is therefore not acceptable if it cannot produce at least 15 percent returns.

The estimated annual returns for each alternative are discounted for the five years, and the present value of the returns for each alternative is compared with the corresponding investment. A table of present values of $1.00 received annually shows that at a 15 percent discount rate, $3.352 is the equivalent of $1.00 received each year for 5 years.

Alternative B is the better candidate for investment at a 15 percent discount rate as shown by the computations given below.

Investment Alternatives

	A	B
Present value of annual returns:		
3.352 x $14,000	$46,928	
3.352 x $25,000		$83,800
Less present value of investment	35,000	70,000
Excess present value of returns over investment	$11,928	$13,800

It may seem that Alternative A is better than Alternative B because Alternative A can produce better returns in relation to the amount invested. The rate that is earned by the investment candidate, however, is not important in decision making. The objective is to select the best candidate, not to compute the rate that is earned by each one. Furthermore, it must be remembered that all future returns are to be reinvested at the minimum rate of 15 percent. In this case, both candidates are superior—each is able to earn more than the minimum rate. The assumption is that the returns will be reinvested to earn 15 percent. Therefore the company will have more capital in future years by selecting Alternative B; that is, of course, if the assumption is correct with respect to the minimum rate of return.

Looking at it in another way, the investment in Alternative B is larger and the returns are also larger. Evaluation can then be made on the basis of the incremental returns in relation to the incremental investment. Is the larger investment justified by the larger returns? In this case, at a 15 percent rate, the incremental investment is justified as shown below.

Investment Alternatives

	A	B	Incremental investment and returns
Annual returns	$14,000	$25,000	$11,000
Present value of annual returns at 15 percent	$46,928	$83,800	$36,872
Less present value of investment	35,000	70,000	35,000
Excess present value of returns over investment	$11,928	$13,800	$ 1,872

The method of evaluating investments just described above is called the *excess present value method.* The present value of the investment is subtracted from the present value of the returns, and the most acceptable candidate for investment on an economic basis is the one that produces the greatest excess. This method can be used to compare investments of different amounts and with different life spans.

Seemingly, investments that will not terminate at the same time cannot be compared unless some provision is made to equate the time periods. For example, a 10-year investment may produce a greater excess of returns over the investment on a present value basis than a 5-year investment. But the time periods aren't equal. After the 5-year investment has been terminated, how much can be earned during the second 5-year period? Perhaps greater returns can be earned with two 5-year investments than from one 10-year investment. However, the assumption has been made that *future returns can be reinvested at the minimum acceptable rate of return.* Therefore, when the returns have been discounted at the minimum acceptable rate, a valid comparison can be made—a difference in time periods notwithstanding. A reinvestment of the returns from the 5-year investment is expected to earn additional returns at the minimum acceptable rate. Thus the reinvested returns and the additional returns from reinvestment on a present value basis will cancel out. Or any additional investment made at the end of the first 5-year period will be canceled out by the present value of the returns for the next 5 years.

It may also be argued that net working capital returns are not necessarily received at the end of each year but, instead, flow in during the year. Hence, a present value factor should not be chosen from a table prepared on the basis of annual returns. The annual rate, however, is satisfactory if the pattern of returns is the same for all of the investment candidates under consideration. The objective is to select the best candidate, and this can be accomplished as well with an annual rate as with a continuous rate, provided that the pattern of returns during the year is the same for all candidates.

An investment decision is not a decision to be made at one time and then forgotten. The investment planning operation should be continuous. Past investments should be reevaluated periodically by comparing the actual net working capital returns as realized with the original estimates. If the actual returns are unsatisfactory, it may be possible to determine the underlying causes and to make corrections. Perhaps it will be found that the investment should never have been made, in which case it may be better to dispose of it before losses or unsatisfactory returns accumulate further. The practice of reviewing the results from past investments is a highly important part of managerial control. Furthermore, the experience gained from this review helps management to make better investment decisions in the future.

A GRAPHIC PRESENTATION

If desired, the capital investment comparison can be shown on a graph that is somewhat similar to the P/V graph used in profit planning. Various discount rates are shown on the horizontal scale, and a horizontal line drawn above the base line serves as a break-even line. The excess of returns over the investment on a present value basis is depicted on the vertical scale above this line, and a deficiency of returns is depicted below this line.

The data from the previous example are used again for a graphic presentation.

Investment Alternatives

	A	B
Net investment	$35,000	$70,000
Estimated annual returns for each of 5 years	14,000	25,000

In the previous example, when returns were discounted at an assumed minimum rate of 15 percent, Alternative B was the better investment candidate. The graph given below shows that the selection of an investment candidate depends in part upon the minimum rate of return.

The computations used in the preparation of the following graph are given below.

Alternative A

Discount rates	Present value of returns	Investment	Excess (or deficiency) of returns
5	$60,260	$35,000	$25,620
10	53,074	35,000	18,074
15	46,928	35,000	11,928
20	41,874	35,000	6,874
25	37,646	35,000	2,646
30	34,104	35,000	(896)

Alternative B

Discount rates	Present value of returns	Investment	Excess (or deficiency) of returns
5	$108,250	$70,000	$38,250
10	94,775	70,000	24,775
15	83,800	70,000	13,800
20	74,775	70,000	4,775
25	67,225	70,000	(2,775)
30	60,900	70,000	(9,100)

The graph in Figure 12-1 clearly shows that if returns can be reinvested at a rate of between 15 and 20 percent, a point of indifference is reached. The lines for the investment candidates cross at this point, and one candidate is as acceptable as the other. At discount rates lower than this break-even point, Alternative B is the better candidate and at higher discount rates, Alternative A is better.

Another break-even point is reached for each investment candidate when the zero line is crossed. The line for Alternative B crosses the zero line betweeen 20 and 25

A Capital Investment Graph

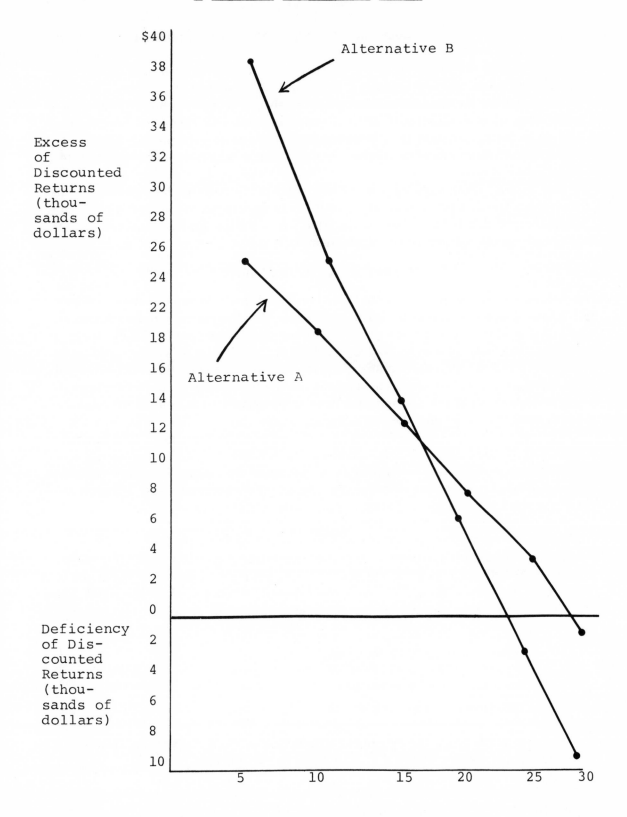

Figure 12-1

percent and is no longer even an acceptable candidate beyond that point, and Alternative A becomes unacceptable at a discount rate of almost 30 percent.

In comparing investment candidates, the graph can be most helpful by showing a wide range of possibilities with different discount rates. One candidate, for example, will be a better selection if it is anticipated that future returns may have to be reinvested at lower rates while another candidate will be better when rates are expected to be higher.

One form of break-even point is reached when the lines for each investment candidate cross. This is a point of indifference in choosing between candidates. A candidate should not be selected at or beyond the point where the line for that candidate crosses the break-even line drawn on the graph—the zero line.

A SALE AS AN INVESTMENT

Generally, a decision to sell is not looked upon as being a decision to invest. Instead, it is viewed as a disinvestment. The sale, however, like the purchase is an investment; and this is apparent when the sales transaction is examined more closely. When a decision has been made to sell any productive asset, the seller has apparently considered that the proceeds from the sale are worth more to him than the discounted returns that he could obtain by holding the asset. On the other hand, if he refuses to sell, he believes that the discounted returns to be derived from holding the asset are worth more than he could obtain by selling the asset.

The proceeds to be derived from the sale are like the investment in a purchase situation. If these proceeds are sacrificed by holding the asset, the sacrifice or opportunity cost is the investment in a continued operation. The future returns expected from the asset are discounted at the minimum acceptable rate of return and are compared with the proceeds that can presently be derived from its sale.

Assume, for example, that a piece of equipment in present operation can be sold for $80,000 net of income tax on any gain or loss arising from the sale. According to estimates made, this equipment should yield net working capital returns after income taxes of $30,000 each year for the next 5 years, and the minimum acceptable rate of return is 20 percent. Should the equipment be sold or continued in operation? The analysis given below shows that the equipment more than meets the rate-of-return objective.

Annual returns of $30,000 for 5 years discounted at 20 percent (2.991 x $30,000)	$89,730
Proceeds from sale (the investment)	80,000
Excess returns on a present value basis	$ 9,730

In the example given, the equipment should be continued in operation. However, if the discounted returns were not at least equal to the proceeds from sale of $80,000, the equipment should be sold.

Sometimes investment decisions involving a sale are made involuntarily by neglect. Opportunities for sale may be overlooked, and an asset may be held even if, in some cases, it should be sold. Or the cost initially invested in the asset (the sunk cost) may be an obstacle that is incorrectly allowed to cloud the decision. Perhaps the asset should be sold, but the seller hesitates because of the amount that he originally invested. He doesn't like to accept the fact that he may be better off by selling at a loss. The original mistake is unfortunate, but another mistake should not be made because of it.

The proper approach is to look to the future, not to the past. Compare the present value of the expected returns from continued operation with the amount that can be obtained from selling the asset. Forget the costs that were incurred in the past. These costs have no bearing on the future.

SUMMARY

The capital investment decision is one of the most important decisions facing business management. This is true because often the amount to be invested is substantial, and a decision will often influence the course of operations for several years to come. The capital investment decision is also a difficult decision, depending as it does upon reasonably accurate estimates projected well into the future.

The mechanical process of selecting the best investment candidate from among those that are available is not difficult. Essentially, the decision-making problem is a break-even problem. The returns expected from each investment alternative are discounted at the lowest acceptable rate of return and are compared with the corresponding investment that is similarly stated on a present value basis. If the two amounts are equal, a break-even point has been reached. The best candidate from an economic standpoint is the one that produces the largest excess of returns over the investment on a present value basis.

13

Maintaining Balance
in the Capital Structure

In the preceding chapters, the break-even concept was applied for the most part in selecting the most profitable course of action in conducting operations. In some cases, it was a matter of reducing costs to a minimum or obtaining the best possible revenues, and in other cases the problem was to obtain the best combination of revenues and costs. In the preceding chapter attention was directed to the selection of the best capital investment candidate for an investment situation. However, very little has been said up to this point about how to obtain the funds that are needed to finance the investments—the investments that in turn are expected to produce the profits.

In Chapter 12 it was pointed out that a capital investment alternative is selected from among those that are available for a given purpose without including the costs of financing. This does not mean that the financing costs are unimportant and can be disregarded—far from it. It does mean that, as a general rule, the candidates for a given investment situation are rated on the basis of their relative profitability without regard to the costs of financing. The assumption is that the same financing arrangements can be made for all candidates with no difference in the rates. As is the case with all general rules, there are exceptions. For example, if the amount to be invested in one candidate is considerably larger than the amount to be invested in a competing candidate, there may be an effect on the costs of financing. If this is true, the additional cost of financing should be included in making the investment decision.

While the costs of financing are usually not included in selecting the best candidate for an individual investment situation, they are highly relevant in planning the *total* capital investment program. Plans to increase the total capital investment are governed to a large extent by the expected profitability of investments, by the amount of money that can be obtained, and by the cost of that money. As the costs of financing increase, the importance of making sound investment decisions also increases.

When additional investment projects are added to build up a total investment plan, the costs of financing may also increase. Investment projects will be assigned priorities, and at some point projects that offer low profit returns relative to the costs to finance them will have to be eliminated from the total plan. This decision in itself is a break-even type of decision.

In this chapter, however, attention is directed to the various ways of financing the assets of the business and the ways to maintain or to restore balance in the equity structure. Stated more directly, the objective is to balance the equity structure in order to minimize the overall cost of capital.

SOURCES OF CAPITAL

It is a gross oversimplification to say that there are two basic sources of capital: capital obtained from those who do not own the business and capital obtained from those who do. These two sources of capital are designated in a corporation as:

1. Debt (outsiders)
2. Stockholders' equity (owners of a corporation).

Within each of these broad categories there are distinctions and refinements. A few of the major distinguishing features will be outlined briefly.

DEBT EQUITY

The equities of those who extend credit to a corporation can be classified generally as follows:

1. Short-term debt
   (a) no cost (free)
   (b) with interest cost
2. Long-term debt (with interest cost)

Short-Term Debt

Short-term debt, both the free debt and the debt with interest cost, is a part of the total capital structure. Virtually every business enterprise has the use of a limited amount of capital for a very short time at no cost. For example, materials and services are rendered with the expectation that payment will be made in the very near future. The liability for future payments is entered under accounts payable, wages payable, income taxes payable, or some other descriptive caption to denote the nature of the liability. Also there is a certain time lag in receiving and disbursing monies because of bank clearing operations. In general, no interest is charged for credit granted to others on the same terms. Customers of the business are ordinarily not charged interest on accounts receivable.

Short-term loans may be obtained from banks or other lending institutions to finance inventories or operations. These loans bear interest and usually mature in a few months. Normally a company that has a temporary need for funds to finance operations during a portion of its operating cycle will establish a permanent relationship with a bank or banks so that resources up to a certain amount can be obtained when needed.

Short-term debt is an important part of the total capital structure, but like the current assets that it finances, it circulates rapidly with no particular debt extending beyond a few months. There may be circumstances where long-term projects or capital assets are financed on the short-term money market with the debt being renewed from time to time as it becomes due. Short-term financing of long-term assets, however, is unusual and may sometimes be employed to obtain funds at favorable terms while waiting for better opportunities to enter the long-term capital market.

Long-Term Debt

As a rule, capital investments are financed either by long-term debt or by resources furnished by the stockholders. The more or less permanent part of the capital structure will be discussed throughout the remainder of this chapter, bearing in mind of course that the composite cost of capital is a mixture of the costs that can be identified with *all* segments of the capital structure.

Long-term debt is a relative term. What is long term? Is it two years? Three years? Five years? Ten? What are the limits? In conventional accounting practice, debt that becomes due more than a year later is classified as long-term debt. Obviously, there is a distinction between debt that becomes due in two or three years and debt that does not become due for 20 years. And this distinction will be reflected in the interest rates. The general approach in determining the cost of long-term debt will be the same in any case; to simplify the discussion these refinements will not be discussed.

Long-term debt differs from stockholders' equity in many important respects.

1. The holder of debt is an outsider and does not share the risks, responsibilities, and privileges of ownership.
2. Debt matures at a stated time in the future, and sometimes a provision is made for retirement before the maturity date.
3. Interest is accumulated at a given rate and is often paid in quarterly or semiannual installments.
4. Properties of the firm may or may not be pledged to support the debt.
5. Sometimes debt is issued with a conversion privilege that allows the holder to convert the debt to common stock under given terms.

Ordinarily, long-term debt is issued under an agreement called an indenture that sets forth terms for the protection of the creditor and the firm. For example, while the debt is outstanding, there may be restrictions on the amount that can be paid to the stockholders as dividends, or there may be certain financial ratios that must be maintained. A provision may also be included to declare the debt in default if some requirement is not met, with further provisions specifying what action will be taken in that event.

Long-term leases for many years have been looked upon as rental agreements that are somehow apart from debt. In more recent years the long-term lease agreement has been more correctly viewed as a variation of conventional long-term financing. The obligation to make periodic rental payments over a period of years is virtually the same as paying interest and principal on debt. Included in the lease payments is an interest cost that is the cost of capital—the cost to have the use of the resources obtained under lease. If, for any reason, the lease is canceled before the termination date, there may be cancellation penalties. Conventional long-term debt agreements may also include provisions for premiums to be paid in the event of premature retirement. These provisions in lease and debt agreements should be considered in the evaluation of financing arrangements.

OWNERS' EQUITY

The interests of the stockholders in a corporation are subordinate to the interests of the holders of debt. The return on the stockholders' investment is relatively uncertain when compared with the return on debt equity. The return, if any, depends upon the earnings of the corporation. There is no property pledged to protect the stockholders. They must accept whatever remains after the claims of all other equity holders have been satisifed. The stockholder is an owner and as such assumes the risks of the business. He may lose the amount he invested, or he may receive much more than he invested if the corporation prospers.

Preferred Stock

The preferred stock often lies in a twilight zone between debt and owners' equity. Often it is protected from risk to some extent, but it is still considered to be a part of owners' equity and is classified as such. Preferred stock may have no established maturity date, but dividends are specified at a set rate—a rate that must be paid before dividends are distributed on the common stock. In addition, the preferred stock agreement may include a provision for sharing dividends with the common stock after the preference dividend is paid. If the corporation is dissolved or if the preferred stock is to be retired, the preferred stockholders may be given preference over the common stockholders. In some cases, preferred stock may be converted to common stock under certain specified terms. The preferred stockholders, in exchange for special privileges, may be given only limited voting rights.

A corporation may have two or more classes of stock outstanding with no particular class being designated as preferred or common. An examination of the stock agreements, however, will reveal the classes of stock that are preferred because of special privilege, and the class of stock that bears the ultimate risk of ownership is essentially the common stock.

Common Stock

The equity of the common stockholders is the residual equity. After the claims of all other equity holders have been satisifed, the common stockholders receive their share. The common stockholders are exposed and may lose a portion or all of their investment. If the company is successful, however, the other equity holders will receive only the stipulated return on their investments while the common stockholders receive the benefits of above-average profits.

There is a cost of financing with resources obtained from common stockholders even though the cost is not stated explicitly. In the case of debt, the interest cost can usually be determined without much difficulty, and with preferred stock there is the established preference dividend rate. The cost of common stock financing is much more difficult to determine, depending as it does upon the relationship between expected future earnings and the market price of the stock.

The reinvested earnings also have a cost. Earnings are either distributed as dividends, or they are reinvested to earn future returns. In either case, the investing public evaluates the effect by placing a market value on the stock. It may be argued that dividends are taxable to the investor and that this must be considered. Individual investors will take this into account when establishing a market value for the stock. From the point of view of the corporation, however, the cost of capital is determined by the investors' appraisal of the relationship between future dividends and future growth of earnings to the market price of the stock. The cost of capital for the corporation is then established in the market place and probably is influenced by taxes imposed upon the various investors, but the corporation has no control over the factors used by investors in making an evaluation.

DEBT FINANCING

The cost to finance with debt is relatively easy to determine inasmuch as debt has a stated return. The interest rate specified for the debt issue is referred to as the nominal rate of return and is a starting point in determining the true interest cost.

An example is given to show how the true or effective interest rate can be computed. Assume that bonds maturing in ten years at $10,000,000 pay interest at the rate of 7 percent per year. Conditions in the money market may be such that the investors will want more than a 7 percent yield, in which case the bonds will be sold for less than their face value—the additional interest requirement being satisfied by the differential between the face value of the bonds and the amount that the investors will pay for them. Conversely, if the investors are more than satisfied with the nominal interest rate, the bonds will be sold at a premium—the excess over par operating to reduce the true interest cost.

Furthermore, the cost of issuing the bonds must be deducted from the gross proceeds to obtain the *net* amount available to the company for investment. The cost of debt capital to the company is the rate of interest on this net amount.

Assume, in this case, that the company receives $8,700,000 from the bond issue after deducting all costs of placing the issue with the investing public. Bond yield tables show that these bonds have an effective yield of approximately 9 percent, and this is the cost of this particular segment of debt. If bond yield tables are not available, the effective interest rate is the discount rate that discounts the periodic interest payments and the amount to be paid upon retirement of the debt to a present value that is equal to the amount received upon issuance of the debt. In this example, with a 9 percent discount rate a payment of $10,000,000 at the end of 10 years plus 10 annual payments of $700,000 is approximately equivalent to a present payment of $8,700,000.

Interest on debt is deductible for income taxes; if the corporate income tax rate is 50 percent, an interest cost of 9 percent before taxes becomes 4-1/2 percent after taxes. Interest on debt offers a tax advantage to the corporation, whereas dividends to stockholders are a distribution of earnings and cannot be deducted in computing income taxes.

Leverage

Debt financing can be used to enhance the rate of return to the owners. If capital furnished by outsiders earns more than it costs, the excess return goes to the owners. This advantage of debt financing is spoken of as *leverage.* The borrowed capital, by earning more than it costs, acts as a lever to produce more earnings for the owners. On the other hand, if the borrowed capital earns less than it costs, the earnings for the owners are reduced.

The principle of leverage can be illustrated by assuming that a corporation is formed and that all of the capital of $100,000 has been furnished by the stockholders. The profit after income taxes for the first year amounts to $15,000, and the stockholders earn a 15 percent return on their investment.

Assume, however, that instead of investing the entire $100,000 themselves, the stockholders invest only $50,000 and borrow the other $50,000 at an interest cost of 8 percent before income taxes. If income taxes are at the rate of 50 percent, the interest rate after taxes if 4 percent. The profit after income taxes, without considering the interest cost, is $15,000, as it was before. The stockholders, however, now earn 26 percent on their investment.

	Total	Debt	Stock
Capital structure	$100,000	$50,000	$50,000
15% profit after taxes	$ 15,000	$ 7,500	$ 7,500
Less 4% interest after taxes	2,000	2,000	—
Profit for stockholders	$ 13,000	$ 5,500	$ 7,500

Rate of return to stockholders:

$$\frac{\$13,000 \text{ profit}}{\$50,000 \text{ stockholders' equity}} = 26\%$$

The stockholders not only earn the 15 percent return derived from their own investment, but they also receive the return on the borrowed capital that is in excess of the interest cost. As a result, the rate of return on the amount invested by the stockholders is increased.

With the advantage of leverage and the tax deduction for interest, it may appear that debt financing should always be favored. But the tendency to finance with debt must be restrained. As debt is increased, risk increases.

With increased risk, lenders will charge higher interest rates and impose more stringent restrictions in the indentures. Furthermore, a firm that has borrowed beyond prudent limits will have a lower credit rating than a firm that has maintained balance in the equity structure. Investors who are permitted by law to buy only top grade securities may not be able to buy the securities, and this will limit the available market. As a result, the firm may have difficulty in obtaining new capital, perhaps at a time when the need is great. When the risk is considered to be substantial, the common stock will sell for less, reflecting the anxiety of the market with respect to risk. The cost to finance with either debt or stock will then be higher than it would be if balance were maintained.

While borrowing has its advantages, it must be held within reasonable limits with debt and stock being held in proper proportions. An astute financial manager tries to hold a point of balance, financing as needed with either debt or stock to maintain this balance, thereby reducing the combined cost of capital to a minimum.

The judicious use of leverage and the various methods of financing are highly significant factors in determining the cost of capital. As stated before, plans to increase the total capital investment depend upon the expected profitability of the investments. And the profitability of the investments in the final analysis will be enhanced or depressed by the quality of the financing decisions and the balance in the company's financial structure.

THE OWNERS' INVESTMENT

The cost of the segment of capital furnished by the preferred stockholders is relatively easy to compute, as a rule, and for that reason will be discussed first. Under normal conditions the holders of preferred stock anticipate a certain return in dividends each year with no specified termination date. Thus the stated dividend per share expressed as a percentage of the market value per share is the cost of preferred capital stock. In more unusual circumstances where the preferred stock agreement provides for variations in the return, the cost of capital will depend upon the expectations of the market with respect to the return in relation to the going market price. If this is the case, the cost of capital will be computed in much the same way as it is for common stock.

The cost of the common stock is more difficult to determine because of greater uncertainty. The market price of the stock depends upon the investors' evaluation of future dividends and the growth of earnings. The future anticipated earnings when discounted to a present value become the market value of the stock.

Common stock to the investor is an asset; like any other asset, its value is the discounted flow of future earnings that it can be expected to produce. Expectations may be disappointed, but at any given time the market places a value upon an asset, a value that is derivied from estimates of future earning power. Note that the *future* holds the key to value, not the past. Past results may be a guide in predicting the future, but assets are purchased in anticipation of future returns, not past returns.

Common stock, unlike many other assets, does not have a limited life. It is assumed that the stream of expected returns will continue into the future indefinitely or, at the very least, for an undefined interval of time.

From the point of view of the corporation, the cost of common stockholders' equity is based upon the investors' expectations with respect to future dividend yield and growth of earnings.

No Growth Expected

Assume, for example, that investors anticipate that the earnings of a certain company will amount to $5.00 a share and that all of these earnings will be paid out in dividends. No growth of earnings is expected, and an investor who buys this stock buys it to obtain a $5.00 return each year.

If the market price of the stock is $50, the investor is receiving a 10 percent return on his investment and the price earnings ratio is 10.

Rate of return:

$$\frac{\$5.00 \text{ annual dividend}}{\$50.00 \text{ market price of stock}} = 10\%$$

Price-earnings ratio:

$$\frac{\$50.00 \text{ market price of stock}}{\$5.00 \text{ annual dividend}} = 10.$$

The rate of return to the investor is 10 percent, and the cost of capital to the firm is also 10 percent assuming that there are no costs of financing.

If a new issue of stock is placed on the market, the corporation may receive $45 after deducting the underwriters' commission and other costs. The cost of capital then becomes 11.1 percent.

Cost of capital:

$$\frac{\$5.00 \text{ annual dividend}}{\$45.00 \text{ net proceeds from issue of stock}} = 11.1\%$$

The cost of capital may change, however, if the market reevaluates the earnings potential and the risk of the firm or if there is any change that will have an effect on the money market. Suppose that the market wants more than a 10 percent return on an investment that yields $5.00 a year. The market price of the stock may decline to $40 with the rate of return and the cost of capital to the corporation (leaving out the costs of financing) increasing to 12.5 percent.

Cost of capital:

$$\frac{\$5.00 \text{ annual dividend}}{\$40.00 \text{ market price of stock}} = 12.5\%$$

Growth Expected

With an estimated growth of earnings, additional uncertainty is introduced. The investor must not only anticipate a stream of dividends, but he must also estimate a rate of growth in earnings. The price that he is willing to pay for the stock is based upon his evaluation of the future dividends that he will receive and the appreciation of the value of the stock resulting from growth in earnings.

The rate of return to the investor or the cost of capital from the corporate point of view is then equal to the relationship of the expected dividend plus the expected rate of growth to the market price of the stock. For example, assume that a $5.00 dividend per share is expected next year and that 50 percent of the earnings each year are to be paid out in dividends. Furthermore, the market expects earnings to grow at the rate of 5 percent a year. If the stock sells for $100 a share, it yields 10 percent to the investor; and the cost of capital is also 10 percent.

Dividend return:

$$\frac{\$5.00 \text{ dividend}}{\$100.00 \text{ market price of stock}} = 5\%$$

Rate of growth expected $= 5\%$

Cost of capital (rate of return) $\underline{10\%}$

This approach can be illustrated by projecting the estimated results for five years into the future as shown below.

Years	Market price, beginning of year	Earnings per share	Dividends per share	Total returns
1	$100.00	$10.00	$5.00	$5.00
2	105.00	10.50	5.25	5.25
3	110.25	11.02	5.51	5.51
4	115.70	11.57	5.78	5.78
5	121.50	12.15	6.07	6.07
6	127.60			

Proceeds received from the sale of the stock at the end of five years   127.60

Total returns $155.21

The returns when discounted at 10 percent are equal to $100.00, the original price of the stock. Therefore, the discounted rate of return on the investment or the cost of capital to the corporation is 10 percent.

This will be true whether the returns are projected ahead for 5 years, 10 years, or for any number of years. Five years were arbitrarily selected for the example, but the same rate of return would be derived from projecting the results further into the future.

In the example given, the earnings are expected to grow at a rate of 5 percent a year with half of the earnings paid out in dividends. The investors seek a 10 percent return and place a value of $100 on the stock. Assume, however, that the investors want a 15 percent rate of return. In this case, with everything else being the same, they will place a value of $50 on the stock. To simplify the example even further, results will be projected only *one* year into the future as shown below.

Years	Market price, beginning of year	Earnings per share	Dividends per share	Total returns
1	$50.00	$10.00	$5.00	$5.00
2	52.50 Proceeds received from sale of stock			52.50
			Total returns	$57.50

The stockholder receives a $5.00 dividend and sells the stock at the end of the year for $52.50. His total return when discounted at 15 percent is equal to the price he paid for the stock.

The investor places a value on the stock that will give him the desired dividend rate plus the growth rate as he has projected it.

Price of stock	$50.00

Dividend return:

$$\frac{\$5.00 \text{ dividend}}{\$50.00 \text{ market price of stock}} = 10\%$$

Rate of growth expected	=	5%
Cost of capital (rate of return)		15%

At any time it is assumed that he can sell his stock to obtain an amount that together with the dividends will give him the desired rate of return. In practice, market conditions change, growth rates may be estimated incorrectly, and growth rates may change. At the *present* time, however, the evaluation of the future by the investors places a rate of return on the stock that is also the cost of common stock to the corporation.

A COMBINED COST OF CAPITAL

The combined cost of capital for a firm is the weighted average of the costs of the various individual segments of the capital structure. If the various types of capital are properly blended in the capital structure, the combined cost of capital is minimized.

One of the major objectives of management is to maximize the value of the capital stock over the long run; this can be accomplished by obtaining the best possible profits from operations and by holding the financial costs to a minimum. If too much debt is added to the equity structure, risk increases. Interest cost is then higher than it should be and the value of the stock declines. If the equity of the common stockholders is too large a proportion of the total equity, interest cost may be low, but the market value of the stock is depressed.

The Balanced Firm

The well-established firm over the years may have located the optimum point of balance or an approximately optimum point of balance. A comparison with other companies in the industry together with experience may have helped the firm to achieve a balance. The problem for this type of firm then is not so much a problem of trying to determine where the point of balance lies as it is to maintain this balance. Debt and stockholders' equity will be held at the predetermined proportions, with changes being made as necessary to compensate for outside influences on the market.

In the example given below, the proportions of debt and stockholders' equity are given along with the percentage of cost for each segment of the total capital. The weighted average cost of capital in this example is 9.6 percent.

	Equity Percentage		Cost of capital after income taxes	Weighted cost of capital
Debt	30%	x	4.0%	1.2%
Stock	70	x	12.0	8.4
	100%		Combined cost	9.6%

Assume that the company plans to issue new debt without increasing the stockholders' equity and that this increase in debt will increase the debt percentage to 35 percent. The cost to borrow additional funds may increase, and the price of the stock may decline as shown below.

	Equity percentages	Cost of capital after income taxes	Weighted cost of capital
Debt	35%	4.5%	1.575%
Stock	65	13.0	8.45
	100%	Combined cost	10.025%

Moving in the other direction, assume that the company increases the stockholders' equity from 70 percent to 75 percent. The interest rate may go down, but the market price of the stock may also go down, thus increasing the cost of the stockholders equity.

	Equity percentages		Cost of capital after income taxes	Weighted cost of capital
Debt	25%	x	3.5%	.875
Stock	75	x	15.0	11.25
	100%		Combined cost	12.125

In the example given, a 30:70 mix of debt and stockholders' equity appears to be approximately right. If this is so, the firm will add debt and stockholders' equity in this proportion. Tests may be made to obtain refinements or to see if adjustments should be made. Underwriters and financial analysts may be able to furnish guidance to indicate the direction in which the company should move, and to what extent, in order to maintain the best possible position in the capital market.

The Unbalanced Firm

The firm that is not fortunate enough to have obtained balance in its equity structure may find it somewhat difficult to make the necessary adjustments in its equity structure. The need for adjustments may be obvious, but investors may be slow in giving recognition to a firm that is out of balance. New debt issues, for example, will not be given higher ratings at once, and the stock may not sell at favorable prices until after the firm has established itself properly. Gradually, the combined cost of capital can be reduced by following the lead of the more balanced companies in the industry and by watching for opportunities to improve the equity mix.

The Small Firm

Most of the discussion in this chapter has been centered on the large firm where the stock is actively traded. The small firm is usually at a disadvantage by not having an established national credit reputation. As a result, it may have difficulty in obtaining funds other than from local sources where the reputation of the principal owner will be a big factor.

The closely held corporation—the family-style corporation—will sometimes be in a position where the distinction between debt and stockholders' equity may blur. The principal stockholder may seek the tax advantage of interest deductions by holding a large part of *his* investment in the corporation in the form of debt. The interest can be deducted in computing corporate income taxes and is taxable to the individual as income. This portion of the investment is only taxed once. However, dividends are taxed twice—once as earnings of the corporation and again as dividend income for the individual.

The tax advantage to the owner of holding debt may disappear if the proportion of debt is too high. Tax authorities may deny the interest deduction if the debt was issued primarily as a tax-saving device with no plan for eventual retirement. The so-called interest may be declared to be nothing more than a dividend to the owner.

The principal owner of a closely held corporation is generally reluctant to sell common stock to the public and prefers to finance with debt. If the owner cannot invest additional funds himself, he risks losing control by issuing stock to outside interests. As a result, there is an even greater risk that the closely held corporation will become unbalanced with too much debt. The short-sighted owner may not realize that he can also lose control of his company if he cannot handle the debt properly. From the principal owner's point of view, the cost of the capital that he has invested is the opportunity cost of the returns that he could obtain from an outside investment.

SUMMARY

Corporate capital can be obtained in a variety of ways and under different conditions. In a very broad sense, capital is either obtained from outsiders in the form of debt or from the insiders or owners in the form of stock and reinvested earnings. There is a cost attached to both debt and the owners' investment.

The objective in balancing the equity structure is to hold debt and the owners' investment in proper proportions. The best capital mix is the one that minimizes the cost of capital to the firm. Risk increases when debt is too large in proportion to the total equity, and as a result the cost of capital is higher than it should be. The cost of capital is also higher than it should be when the owners' investment is too large a proportion of the total equity. With too much owners' equity, the firm is not obtaining enough advantage from leverage, and investors will tend to place a lower value on the stock.

Some firms have found an approximate point of balance in the equity structure and will add new capital in this proportion, adjusting when necessary to changing conditions in the capital market. The firms that have not found this balance can work to obtain balance by examining the capital structures of similar companies and by seeking the advice of underwriters.

Part of the problem is to recognize when imbalance exists! This is one reason why it is so important to know how to compute the cost of both debt and owners' equity and to recognize what will probably happen to the combined cost of capital if either debt or owners' equity is increased.

14

Break-Even Applications in the Non-Profit Organization

Ordinarily the break-even point is considered in a very restricted way to be the balancing point between profits and losses. According to this rather narrow definition, break-even analysis has value only as a tool to be used by commercial and industrial entities in profit planning and decision making. Closer examination, however, reveals that the concept of a fulcrum or a point of balance is universal.

Our interest is in economic affairs, but even here no limit has to be imposed by looking exclusively at profits. All of us, acting either as individuals or as members of a group, are subject to the realities of economics—even though we may be engaged in activities where profit is of no importance, and indeed, even when profit is shunned as being evidence of a gross preoccupation with money. Even though profit may have little appeal, the economic factors must be recognized as long as we live in a society where resources are relatively scarce.

A non-profit entity such as a governing unit, a governmental agency, an educational or religious organization, a foundation, a charitable fund, or a social club can use the break-even principle in planning and controlling its activities. The objective of the non-profit type or organization is defined in terms of social welfare or services to society or to a particular segment of society. Decisions will not necessarily depend upon the economic advantage or disadvantage attached to a given course of action, but at the same time economic measurements will play an important part. In any type of undertaking, it is necessary to measure the amount of effort (cost) that is required to attain desired results. A question will often arise as to whether or not a certain stated objective is worth the effort. Or looking at the problem in another way, which projects or activities should be favored when there are limited resources?

A non-profit organization is not primarily concerned with economics and will often sacrifice an economic advantage in order to attain some goal that has been assigned a higher priority than economic success. As stated in earlier chapters, even the commercial type of entity may sometimes sacrifice an alternative that offers the best economic advantage. Throughout society, all types of organizations are becoming increasingly conscious of social needs—needs that are difficult to measure precisely in terms of dollars. For example, it is not easy to measure the value of maintaining the physical and mental health of our population or the value of uplifting society by encouragement of the creative arts. Yet it is important that these measurements be made in deciding what should be done and in assigning priorities for various activities.

A VALUATION PROBLEM

The conventional measurement of the economic advantage or disadvantage of an alternative is important even though the decision may not be based on economic results. Conventional economic measurements can be used to establish values for factors that are not ordinarily measured in economic terms. The measurement of an economic advantage that has been sacrificed becomes a value of an accepted alternative that is difficult to measure in dollars. This value is not necessarily the minimum value or the maximum value, but it is a value that lies within a range of acceptability.

An indirect approach to valuation is quite often employed in business to establish a value in situations where valuation is difficult. For example, capital stock may be issued in exchange for land and buildings. If there is no established market for the stock, the appraised value of the land and buildings is identified as the value of the capital stock.

This same approach can be used to value the projects and activities of a non-profit organization. The opportunity cost—that is, the sacrifice of an economic advantage—becomes a value of the project or activity selected. In addition to the problem of placing values on alternatives, there are other more conventional applications of the break-even concept that apply as much to the non-profit organization as to the commercial type of organization.

GOVERNMENTAL APPLICATIONS

A governmental entity such as a city can apply the break-even principle to spread the tax burden among the citizens in as equitable a manner as possible to obtain the revenue needed for municipal operation. The general practice in government is to prepare a budget of estimated expenditures for the coming fiscal year and to match this budget with a budget of estimated revenues. If the two budgets are too far out of balance, taxes may have to be raised or new sources of taxes considered as a means of obtaining the revenues. Or the budget of expenditures may have to be reduced.

Assume that a budget of expenditures has been prepared and that all revenues from sources other than real estate taxes have been estimated. The desired revenue from real estate taxes can easily be computed from the equation given below.

$$\text{Estimated expenditure} - \begin{array}{l}\text{Estimated revenues}\\\text{from sources other}\\\text{than the real estate}\end{array} = \begin{array}{l}\text{Desired revenue}\\\text{from the real}\\\text{estate tax.}\end{array}$$

If the budget is to be balanced, the real estate taxes will have to be equal to the total expenditures minus the estimated revenue from other sources. The budget estimates may indicate that the property owners will have to assume a larger share of the tax burden than they did in past years.

The Millage Rate

If real estate taxes are to be increased, the new millage rate must be determined—assuming that the assessed values of the properties are to remain the same. The desired revenue from the real estate tax is the result of a millage rate multiplied by the assessed value of the properties.

$$\text{Desired revenue from the real estate tax} = \text{Millage rate} \times \text{Assessed value of the properties.}$$

The right-hand side of the equation can be substituted for the desired revenue in the general equation given above.

$$\text{Estimated expenditures} - \text{Estimated revenues from sources other than the real estate tax} = \text{Millage rate} \times \text{Assessed value of the properties.}$$

Assuming that values have been placed on all other factors, the millage rate can be determined as shown below.

$$\frac{\text{Estimated expenditures} - \text{Estimated revenues from sources other than the real estate tax}}{\text{Assessed value of properties}} = \text{millage rate.}$$

To illustrate, it is assumed that municipal expenditures for a certain city have been estimated at \$6,000,000 for the next fiscal year. Revenue from wage taxes, licenses, fees, and from all other sources aside from real estate taxes have been estimated at \$2,400,000. The total assessed value of properties in the tax base amounts to \$240,000,000. The real estate tax is then expected to produce \$3,600,000 on an assessed valuation of \$240,000,000. Thus, the millage rate must be 15 mills as computed below.

$$\text{15 mills, real estate tax rate} = \frac{\$6,000,000 - \$2,400,000}{\$240,000,000}$$

The problem, while mechanically simple, is not nearly as simple as it appears to be. Millage-rates can be increased, but only up to a point. An increase in the millage rate, at best, is unpopular, and this will be all the more true if there is a sharp increase or if taxpayers have already been subjected to increases in the recent past or have had other new taxes imposed upon them. The problem is further aggravated if taxes are much lower in nearby communities with little apparent difference in the quality and quantity of services offered.

If the millage rate is considered to be too high, property owners may be inclined to let their properties deteriorate in order to obtain a lower assessment, or they may migrate to other tax jurisdictions, leaving the city to taxpayers who are even less able to absorb the costs of city government. In the example given, assume that the millage is to be increased from 12 mills to 15 mills. For a taxpayer who owns a property assessed at $40,000, this represents an annual increase in property taxes of $120. This may or may not be accepted, depending upon circumstances, but at some point a taxpayer may be willing to accept a loss on the sale of his property rather than to endure what he considers to be an intolerable situation with little prospect for improvement. The taxpayers' reaction to increased taxes presents a break-even type of problem that must be faced by taxing authorities, and this problem will be given more attention at a later point in the chapter.

The Assessed Values

Perhaps the tax problem may have to be approached from a different direction. If there is reason to believe that the millage rate should not be increased, attention may be directed to the assessed valuations. An examination of the assessments may indicate inequities. Some types of properties that should be taxed may be exempt, or individual properties within any classification may be assessed too low, with the result that some taxpayers are carrying more than their fair share of the tax burden.

The tax equation can be rearranged in another way to compute the assessed value or properties that will meet the revenue goal with a fixed millage rate. Assume, for example, that the millage rate is to be maintained at 12 mills. If no other changes are to be made, the assessed value of the properties will have to be increased to $300,000,000.

$$\text{\$300,000,000 assessed value of properties} = \frac{\$6,000,000,000 - \$2,400,000}{.012}$$

In the example given with a fixed amount of revenue required from properties to cover expenditures, the city will either have to increase the millage rate to 15 mills or increase the assessed value of the properties to $300,000,000. Neither of these alternatives may be attractive, in which case it may be necessary to cut the expenditure budget.

Reducing Expenditures

A review of budgeted expenditures may reveal that certain functions and activities can be performed satisfactorily at a lower cost. To some extent, perhaps, the tax problem can be relieved by searching for economies of operation.

Also, difficult decisions may have to be made in deciding which projects are more essential than others. Appropriations may be reduced for low priority projects, or some projects may be eliminated entirely. The decisions with respect to priorities will be complicated by a diversity of interests among the taxpayers. What may appear to be a needless activity and a waste of money to one group of taxpayers may be quite essential to another. Looking at the problem from an economic point of view, a balance must be established between the cost identified with the elimination or reduction of a service and the cost of the taxpayers' resistance to higher taxes.

A sacrifice is involved if a service cannot be given or if it must be reduced because of a lack of funds to support it completely. As nearly as possible this sacrifice should be measured, bearing in mind that a large portion of cost may be only indirectly related to the activity itself. For example, a failure to appropriate adequate funds for parks or for a recreation center for young people may mean that an even larger amount will have to be spent to rehabilitate youth and to combat juvenile crime. Or a failure to make critical street repairs may result in higher costs to repave the streets at a later date. All of these factors should be considered and assigned a value insofar as possible, either directly or indirectly.

Also, the costs of taxpayer resistance to increased taxes must be recognized. This cost may not always be evident over a relatively short period of time, but it is nevertheless a factor. In time the citizens may lose confidence in the government and as a result will not give their support to projects that are truly essential to the welfare of the city. In certain school districts, for example, bond issues for new school facilities have been rejected when the facilities were badly needed. Part of this resistance can be attributed to the taxpayers' knowledge of unwise and wasteful expenditures made in the past. Or the more financially able taxpayers may leave a city over a period of years, with the result that the city will decline from a lack of financial support. This particular problem is quite evident in our society today.

While it may be virtually impossible to arrive at precise cost estimates, the break-even approach offers the advantage of bringing together the critical factors that must be considered in making a decision and provides a framework for resolving the known elements, thereby reducing the area of uncertainty.

$$\begin{array}{ccc} \text{Costs identified with} & & \text{Cost identified with an} \\ \text{the sacrifice of a} & = & \text{adverse reaction of tax-} \\ \text{project or a reduction} & & \text{payers to higher taxes} \\ \text{of expenditures} & & \end{array}$$

The balancing point in this situation may not be a true point of indifference. If the cost of taxpayer resistance is at all substantial in relation to the cost of not having the project, the project should not be undertaken. Actually no particular project may be responsible for the tax dilemma. Collectively all projects contribute to the need for a tax increase. But if the projects are rated according to a priority system, the low priority project will be compared with the expected taxpayer reaction. Projects will be eliminated or expenditures reduced while working up the scale of priorities until an acceptable level is reached.

From an economic point of view, it would appear that a cost on one side of the equation should be given the same weight as a cost on the other side of the equation. And this would be true if the costs on both sides of the equation could be determined with equal precision. However, the cost of taxpayer resistance may be like an iceberg—the visible portion being only a relatively small proportion of the total. If some allowance is not made for the unmeasured cost, it will not only be difficult to go ahead with the current project but also other projects that are even more essential may be handicapped. To some extent, the problem of overcoming taxpayer resistance may be a problem of salesmanship. Has the project been defined properly and explained to the taxpayers? For example, the taxpayer may be asked if he would be willing to give his help to a cause that would cost him only $20 in additional taxes per year. Stated in another way, it may be pointed out that if he doesn't extend his help he may very well lose present advantages that will amount to even more than $20 a year.

No general rule can be given for estimating costs that by their very nature are indefinite. Under the circumstances, the best that can be done is to estimate the costs that can be measured more readily and to bring the other factors together, using experience and judgment as a guide. Each governing unit has its own peculiarities that depend to a large extent upon the population mix, past history, physical location, neighboring tax jurisdictions, and the influence of current national social trends. All of these elements must be brought together in decision making.

CHARITABLE FUNDS

The principles of break-even analysis can also be applied in planning drives to obtain funds for charitable, educational, or religious purposes. The various needs for funds are budgeted along with the costs of the campaign itself to determine the required amount of contributions. Stated in another way, the contributions must balance the cost of the projects and the cost of the campaign.

$$\text{Contributions} = \frac{\text{Fixed cost}}{\text{of campaign}} + \frac{\text{Variable cost}}{\text{of campaign}} + \frac{\text{Estimated cost}}{\text{of projects.}}$$

Past experience combined with the general pattern of contributions from fund drives will reveal to some extent the amount of contributions that can be expected from a campaign with a given fixed cost and with costs that will vary according to the number of solicitations. In planning a campaign, it is often found that a large proportion of the total contributions can be obtained from relatively new donors. There may be many small contributors, but the total contribution from this source may be a small percentage of the total funds obtained.

A pattern of contributions may be estimated as follows:

Size of contribution	Number of donors	Total contributions
$1,000 or more	60	$ 175,000
500 - 999	90	80,000
100 - 499	220	30,000
Less than $100	630	15,000
Totals	1,000	$ 300,000

Campaign efforts will be guided according to the expected responses from the various classes of donors. Some donors will be favorably influenced by a campaign that includes special dinners and awards or some form of recognition for large contributions. Still other donors will be inclined to give more if they believe that the costs of the campaign are being held at a minimum level. The cost of a campaign will depend in part upon the extent of solicitation, the forms of appeal, and the length of the drive.

Ordinarily the costs of a campaign are expected to be no more than 15 percent of the funds raised. However, this percentage will vary depending upon the absolute amount to be raised. When relatively large amounts are to be raised, the cost percentage may be as low as 5 or 6 percent. Here, too, is a form of break-even analysis—matching the costs of the campaign against a stipulated percentage of the estimated contributions.

$$\text{Campaign costs} \;=\; \text{Stated percentage of contributions}$$

For example, assume that $10,000,000 has been established as the campaign drive and that the costs to conduct this campaign are not to exceed 6 percent of the contributions. Thus a limit of $600,000 has been placed on campaign expenditures.

$$\frac{\text{Campaign}}{\text{costs}} = \frac{\text{Stated percentage}}{\text{of contributions}}$$

$$\$600{,}000 \qquad 6\% \text{ of } \$10{,}000{,}000$$

Expenditures in excess of $600,000 must be justified by increases in contributions that will maintain the established percentage relationship. If campaign costs are increased by $12,000, then contributions should increase by $200,000 to maintain a 6 percent relationship of costs to contributions. In some cases, it may be found that the percentage is too rigid and that is must be relaxed to attain the campaign goal.

Another balancing point (break-even point) is established in matching the cost of the desired projects with the amount of contributions estimated to be available for various purposes. This problem is similar to the one faced by governmental units in appropriating funds for various purposes. If the contributions cannot be expected to cover the costs of the projects, it will be necessary to scale the projects down on a priority basis or to eliminate one or more of them that have low priorities. Projects will have to be rated according to their advantages, and to a large extent the evaluation will have to be based on somewhat subjective judgments.

THE HUMAN FACTORS

As stated in earlier chapters, the break-even approach to decision making problems provides an orderly system for gathering together the quantitative data that bear on the decisions. Often a decision will not be made solely on the basis of monetary amounts that can be directly measured and compared. Sometimes the factors that are undefined in quantitative terms may be more important than the measureable factors. This will be particularly true for individuals and for organizations where economic considerations are often secondary. Yet the measurement process itself is essential, if for no other reason, because it helps to establish values for the factors that *are* difficult to measure.

The process of valuation may be somewhat subjective, depending as it does upon the value scale of a particular individual or the collective values of a group of individuals. Perhaps it may be helpful in certain situations to build a utility function that will measure the degree of risk that a person will take to achieve a given objective. A scale of values may be established, for example, to measure the magnitude of desire to attain a set goal. Sacrifices in the form of money or effort may be made willingly up to a point and more reluctantly beyond this point until finally no further sacrifice will be made. A utility function may be represented on a graph as shown in Figure 14-1.

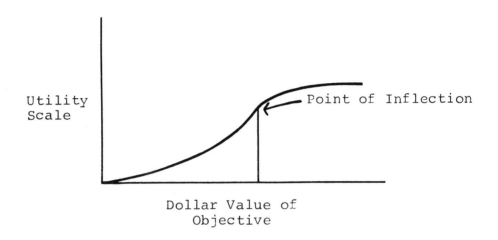

Figure 14-1

The utility function can be expressed as a curve that rises rapidly up to a point that marks the value of the objective in the evaluator's mind. Beyond this point, designated as the point of inflection, the evaluator is less inclined to put forth more effort for additional results. At this point, the slope of the curve changes and eventually levels off.

A utility function is very individualistic, pertaining to only one person and his scale of values. The utility function of one person cannot be compared with the utility function of another. Each person has his own set of values, and his value scale may be established to an extent by scaling his answers to certain questions. For example, would you be willing to give $10 to support a certain project? Would you be willing to give $100, $500, or $1,000 for even better results? In short, how intensely do you desire the success of this project? In setting up a value scale, financial strength must obviously be considered. A $10 contribution from one person may be a real sacrifice, while to another a contribution of $1,000 may involve hardly any sacrifice at all.

A society or a segment of society must reach a compromise on values by deciding collectively on priorities and the amount of effort to be put forth to attain established goals. Break-even analysis in this area extends well beyond conventional analysis and gets into the area of human behavior.

SUMMARY

Entities such as governments and non-profit organizations do not look upon the break-even point as being a balancing point between profits and losses. Instead, the break-even point for these entities is often a balancing point between the cost of desired projects or activities and the resources that can be obtained to cover the cost.

There are certain factors that cannot be measured directly in monetary terms; these factors may be valued indirectly by measuring the extent of monetary sacrifice that will be accepted as a result of their influence. Sometimes subjective valuations can be made from a utility scale to measure the intensity of a person's desire to attain a certain objective. This, too, is an extension of the break-even concept that lies at the heart of decision making.

INDEX

D